These pages are filled with the pain and delight of being a parent, a child, a member of humankind. Their words are like liquid love and tenderness, held together by the bittersweetness of fear and loss. So evocative are these gems, that each twinkles with sparks, that reveal the depth of life. They are reminders of what matters most and they will enchant you and touch your heart.

Emmy van Deurzen, PhD
Professor, New School of Psychotherapy and Counselling at the Existential Academy in London
Author, *Existential Psychotherapy and Counselling in Practice* (3rd ed.) and *Everyday Mysteries* (2nd ed.)

The outstanding Introduction sets the stage for an existential and humanistic immersion into the depths of one of our most impactful and treasured relationships. This extraordinary, heart-centered collection of poignant reflections on the vicissitudes of parenting, being parented, and inclusive family relationships provide intimate glimpses into a nuanced appreciation of the depths of vulnerability, doubt and uncertainty, loss and mourning, the gifts of tenderness and revealing oneself, the delicacy and resilience within life's challenges and growth opportunities; and the power of hope to heal betrayals and breaches with beloved others. A transformative journey into the heart of the relationship.

Shawn Rubin, PsyD
Past-President, Society for Humanistic Psychology
C0-Editor, *Humanistic Psychotherapies: Handbook of Research and Practice*

Lullabies & Confessions: Poetic Explorations of Parenting Across the Lifespan

Edited by
Louis Hoffman
Lisa Xochitl Vallejos

Colorado Springs, CO
www.universityprofessorspress.com

Book Copyright © 2021
The authors of the poems retain the copyright for all poems in this book.

Lullabies & Confessions: Poetic Explorations of Parenting Across the Lifespan
Edited by Louis Hoffman & Lisa Xochitl Vallejos

All rights reserved. No portion of this book may be reproduced by any process or technique without the express written consent of the publisher.

First published in 2021. University Professors Press. United States.

ISBN (print): 978-1-939686-72-5
ISBN (ebook): 978-1-939686-73-2

> University Professors Press
> Colorado Springs, CO
> www.universityprofessorspress.com

Front Cover Image by Lukaya Hoffman
Cover Design by Laura Ross

Reprint permissions listed with the poems.

Dedication

To the parents and children who have touched my life the most deeply....

My sons, Lyon, Lukaya, and Lakoda—you have brought so much laughter and meaning into my life. You have brought an unspeakable love into my life—one that has challenged my love of words to try to bring expression to this love.

My parents, Lynn and Clarence Hoffman—you have modeled love and acceptance in my life and helped me to pass this same love on to my sons. Your love has become my love.

My mothers- and father-in-law: Helen Rahming and Earnal and Stephanie Cleare—thank you for welcoming me to your family and enriching my life. In your witness, I have learned much about parenting and being parented, and I have been blessed by the wisdom.

~ Louis

To Gabriel and Eden, my children. If I had a multitude of words and eternity to speak, I would still never be able to convey the beauty you have brought to my life.

To my parents—each of you brought something different, some dark, some light, but it was all necessary. It was all a gift.

To my brother, Anthony—I watched parenting change you, soften you, and saw the delight on your face being a father. You have shown up for your babies in a way that has been powerful to witness. Thank you for always leading the way.

~ Lisa Xochitl

Poetry, Healing, and Growth Series

Stay Awhile: Poetic Narratives on Multiculturalism and Diversity
Louis Hoffman & Nathaniel Granger, Jr. (Eds.)

Capturing Shadows: Poetic Encounters Along the Path of Grief and Loss
Louis Hoffman & Michael Moats (Eds.)

Journey of the Wounded Soul: Poetic Companions for Spiritual Struggles
Louis Hoffman & Steve Fehl (Eds.)

Our Last Walk: Using Poetry for Grieving and Remembering Our Pets
Louis Hoffman, Michael Moats, and Tom Greening (Eds.)

Poems For and About Elders (Revised & Expanded Edition)
Tom Greening

Connoisseurs of Suffering: Poetry for the Journey to Meaning
Jason Dias & Louis Hoffman (Eds.)

Silent Screams: Poetic Journeys Through Addiction & Recovery
Nathaniel Granger, Jr. & Louis Hoffman

Waterfalls of Therapy
Michael Elliott

A Walk with Nature: Poetic Encounters that Nourish the Soul
Michael Moats, Derrick Sebree, Jr., Gina Subia Belton, & Louis Hoffman

Into the Void: An Existential Psychologist Faces Death Through Poetry
Tom Greening

Poetry, Healing, and Growth Series

The ancient healing art of poetry has been used across cultures for thousands of years. In the Poetry, Healing, and Growth book series, the healing and growth-facilitating nature of poetry is explored in depth through books of poetry and scholarship, as well as through practical guides on how to use poetry in the service of healing and growth. Poetry written with an intention to transform suffering into an artistic encounter is often different in process and style from poetry written for art's sake. This series offers engagement with the poetic greats and literary approaches to poetry while also embracing the beauty of fresh, poetic starts and encouraging readers to embark upon their own journey with poetry. Whether you are an advanced poet, avid consumer, or novice to poetry, we are confident you will find something to inspire your thinking on your personal path toward healing and growth.

Series Editors,
Carol Barrett, PhD; Steve Fehl, PsyD; Nathaniel Granger, Jr., PsyD; Tom Greening, PhD; and Louis Hoffman, PhD

Table of Contents

Acknowledgments	i
Foreword by Barbara Williams & Heather Williams	iii
Introduction	v

Poems — 1

The Light Inside – *Alan King*	3
Icarus's Mother Talks to Her Son - *Lois Marie Harrod*	4
Mother by Any Means - *Ellaraine Lockie*	7
Not My Mother's Daughter – *Lisa Xochitl Vallejos*	9
Every Version – *Louis Hoffman*	11
By What Right? – *Tom Greening*	13
Fear of Heights – *Carol Barrett*	14
The Day She Stopped Telling Me Everything – *Maura Snell*	16
I Hold a Small Death… - *Christina Lovin*	17
Bitties Turning 4 – *Marion Deutsche Cohen*	18
Right Field Siberia – *Charlotte Mandel*	19
The Genes of Guilt – *Patricia Wellingham-Jones*	21
Why I Chose My Parents – *Shoshauna Shy*	23
Ice Storm – *W. F. Lantry*	24
Night Fear – *Charles Rossiter*	26
Definition – *Marilyn Zelke Windau*	27
The Hundred Names of Love – *Annie Lighthart*	28
I Go Back in Time and Rescue My Mother – *Leah Browning*	29
She's Moved to the Other Side of the World – *Phyllis Wax*	31
A Family Affair – *Carol Barrett*	32
Going to Meet Our Birth Daughter After Nineteen Years – *Maura Snell*	34
I Want to Be Ready – *Louis Hoffman*	35
I Never Called Him Foster – *Nathaniel Granger, Jr.*	36
The Catch – *W. F. Lantry*	38
At Jack London State Historic Park – *Shahé Mankerian*	39
The Matter of Smiles – *Marion Deutsche Cohen*	40
My Window – *Evgeny Krayushkin-ZheKa*	42
Learning from the Landscape – *Carol Dorf*	43
Two Balloons – *Michael Moats*	44
Empty Nest– *Michele Riedel*	46

A Mother is Gathering Pens… – *Marilyn Flower*	47
Mother and Son – *Nesreen Frost*	48
Zoe Dances – *Milton J. Bates*	50
Swedish Rye – *Christina Lovin*	51
The Heart's Dark Rooms – *Brenda Yates*	52
Waiting on My Daughter's Night Class – *Carol Barrett*	54
Packing a Box to Send Home from My Daughter's House in Portland – *Shoshauna Shy*	56
Playing in the Sprinkler – *Patricia Wellingham-Jones*	57
Brown Chair – *Louis Hoffman*	58
The Orphan – *Juanita Ratner*	60
Whiskers – *Kimberly Weikert*	61
Haiku for a Wanted Child – *Christina Lovin*	62
Arguing the Curriculum: Coleslaw – *Carol Barrett*	63
Daughter in Her Eighth Month – *Felice Aull*	65
My Father – *Tom Greening*	66
The Glass of Water – *Jeff Santosuosso*	67
At the Doorstep – *John C. Mannone*	69
Every Mother's Son – *Marcella Remund*	70
Next Steps? – *Rodger E. Broomé*	71
Photograph – *Maura Snell*	72
My Father at Ninety-Two, Splitting the Days – *Charlotte Mandel*	73
Necessary Condolences – *Ronnie Hess*	74
By Love – *Veronica Lac*	76
Hydro Superintendent – *Joanne Corey*	78
The Emerald – *Nathaniel Granger, Jr.*	79
My Imperfect Perfect Son – *Louis Hoffman*	81
My Son the Artist – *Michael Harty*	84
Wrenhouse – *W. F. Lantry*	85
How it Feels – *Alan King*	87
That Time Comes – *Patricia Wellingham-Jones*	89
A Heart Attack – *Michael Waterson*	90
A Few Unheard Words – *W. F. Lantry*	91
St. Dominic – *Marcella Remund*	92
What Goes Around – *Ellaraine Lockie*	93
Faerie Panic – *Daniel Ari*	94
Four Months – *Alan King*	95
Risk – *Maura Snell*	97
The Art of War – *Shahé Mankerian*	98
Bird-Boy: Eve Remembering Abel – *Charlotte Mandel*	99

Insomnia Immediately Post-Partum – *Marion Deutsche Cohen*	101
Inside, Looking Out – *Felice Aull*	102
Counterpoint – *Carol Barrett*	103
Brushing My Mother's Teeth – *Christina Lovin*	105
The Mother of the Bride Smiles – *Phyllis Wax*	107
Daddy–Daughter Dance - *Lisa Xochitl Vallejos*	108
The Night He Broke His Collarbone- *Leah Browning*	109
Binky Bond – *Marilyn Zelke Windau*	112
Light Rain – *Annie Lighthart*	113
Skating with Our Daughter on Veteran's Day – *Carol Barrett*	114
Crossing from One Continent to the Next – *Leah Browning*	116
Fruit of Stories – *Carol Dorf*	118
The Child – *Juanita Ratner*	119
The Talk – *Louis Hoffman*	121
Walk – *Marilyn Zelke Windau*	124
The Message – *Annie Lighthart*	125
Morning, Third Sunday in June – *Phyllis Wax*	126
Photograph, 1975 – *Christina Lovin*	127
My Mother's Power – *Felice Aull*	128
The Smell of Pine – *John C. Mannone*	129
Private Enterprise – *Marion Deutsche Cohen*	130
Sleeping Child – *Charlotte Mandel*	131
Watch – *Maura Snell*	132
Mom Raps Me on the Knuckles - *Lois Marie Harrod*	133
Comforting Jack When He Wakes Coughing and Crying with a Cold - *Charles Rossiter*	134
Sea Creatures – *Patricia Wellingham-Jones*	135
After She Tells You – *Maura Snell*	136
The College of Mothers – *Shoshauna Shy*	137
The Interview – *Michele Riedel*	138
Father Hunger – *Michael J. Gargano*	139
Return – *W. F. Lantry*	141
Rehearsals – *Brenda Yates*	142
Impelled Toward Light – *Carol Barrett*	144
Winning Ways – *Carl "Papa" Palmer*	147
Night Fears – *Louis Hoffman*	148
Poetry Activities	151
About the Editors	155

Acknowledgements

Most importantly, we would like to thank the many contributors to this volume who were patient with the slow-moving process of getting this book published. The book is coming to fruition several years after the initial call for poems due to the various ways that life has happened since we began visioning this book.

First, I (Louis) would like to acknowledge my own parents, Clarence and Lynn Hoffman, for being amazing parents and grandparents who have blessed me and my family in many ways. When I was growing up, I vividly remember my father telling my brother and I that they were not perfect parents and encouraging us to be open to reflecting—in therapy if helpful—on how their parenting impacted us. Although I think they did a marvelous job, this permission and encouragement has had a deep, lasting impact upon me that has made me a better parent, spouse, professor, and therapist. Next, I want to thank my parenting partner, Heatherlyn Hoffman. Heatherlyn is a wonderful parent and spouse. I know my children are deeply blessed to have her as a mother, as I am to have her as a wife and partner. And she has tolerated and supported my need to write, including all the long hours of writing and editing. I want to thank my three sons: Lakoda, Lukaya, and Lyon. You have blessed me in so many ways! I also would like to thank John Hoffman, Joy Hoffman, Brittany Garrett-Bowser, and Glen Moriarty, who have been wonderful friends and supporters of my writing. I would like to acknowledge Theopia Jackson and Nathaniel Granger, who have been influential on my writing and learning how to raise biracial children in today's complicated world. Last, I would like to thank Shawn Rubin, Michael Moats, and Jason Dias, who are continual sources of support and encouragement with regards to writing.

I (Lisa Xochitl) would like to thank my ancestors, who bravely fought on so that someday, I would live. My father used to tell me that I have the blood of Indigenous warriors and Spanish conquistadores in my veins, and while that is a complicated history, it is one that has enriched my life. I thank my parents, who were tasked with the job of raising a budding wild woman with a lot to say and a fiery disposition. It wasn't easy, but we made it. To my children, Gabe and Eden; we have been through a lot, and we have done it together, with grace. I am grateful to be your mama. I'd do it all again for one laugh with you.

I would like to acknowledge all of the waymakers in my life; Louis Hoffman, Shawn Rubin, David St. John, Sandy Sela-Smith, Donna Rockwell, and all of the people who believed in me before I believed in myself. You gave me wings.

To my friends, who have become family that are too many to name and my community:

> "Though we tremble before uncertain futures
> may we meet illness, death and adversity with strength
> may we dance in the face of our fears."
> — Gloria Anzaldúa

Foreword

This is a profound and beautiful collection of poetry about parenting across the lifespan.

When a child knows that they are loved and valued for themselves and not for what they do or do not do they have self-confidence and resilience. This book shows the importance of children being able to express their feelings and emotions in a clear straight-way and how this helps them as adults.

This collection of poetry conveys the feelings of both being a child and a parent and captures the importance of self-awareness and the possibilities for change. Reading these poems helps us realize how in our own lives parenting was passed down from great grandparents to grandparents to our parents. They provide insights, profound and beautiful, into who we are today.

Being parented in a positive way helps children learn that they can trust themselves, the world, and other people, and feel confident to explore themselves and know the direction that they would like to go. It can help the child trust different ways of doing things and appreciate differences in people, situations, and other cultures.

This book is invaluable for expecting parents or anyone who is thinking of adding a child to their family and offers ideas of how they want to parent. The poems often show how children remember things and how important it is for parents to respect their child as an individual who has their own ideas from a very early age. Involvement with nature is very helpful in developing the child's awe and curiosity. Sharing these experiences with their parents helps children keep these qualities as they grow.

Engaging to the reader, this collection of poetry offers deep insights into personal growth and awakens memories within us of our own childhood and of our parents.

Barbara Williams, MSW, ACSW
Heather Williams, BSW
Kids' Workshop™
Staff of the Person-Centered Institute of Italy
www.kids-workshop.com

Introduction:
Poetry and Parenting

Poetry is a powerful portal that can help us delve more deeply into understanding ourselves, life, and the world that surrounds us. In this volume, we are using poetry to explore the experience of parenting from both the vantage of having been parented and being a parent.

This book was not constructed as a solely book of art, though it is primarily comprised of art. The book was designed to facilitate a deeper, experiential exploration of being parented and parenting. We hope that you laugh, cry, and reflect through this book. We hope that you are inspired by the art, and that you are prompted to sit with your relationships with your parents and your children.

As you begin this journey into exploring parenting and being parented, we encourage you take a few moments to open yourself up to your own experience each time you sit down to read these poems. This may be through a brief meditation exercise in which you take a few deep breathes and notice what is present in your body. As you do this, try to let go of any expectation from what you are about to read or how you will react to it. As we, the editors, are both existential psychologists, the lens of existential theory and practice influenced how approached writing this book. One of the lessons from existential psychology is that all emotions at their base are healthy. While there are many routes to experiencing emotions in problematic or destructive ways, often it is our confusion, unwillingness to listen, and avoidance of emotions that transform them into various pathologies that impede our ability to experience psychological well-being and live our life as we desire. If we can learn to listen to our emotions with curiosity, instead of resisting them, we begin to recognize the wisdom in our emotions. Through preparing yourself to be open to your experience before you begin reading you can prepare yourself to take in the wisdom of your experience.

Being Parented

Our first experience with parenting is being parented. These formative early experiences have a profound impact on how our life will develop.

As adults, it is critical that we take the time to reflect upon experience of being parented, especially before becoming a parent.

Being Parented as a Portal to Self-Awareness
The evolving relationship we have with our parents can be a powerful tool for learning about ourselves. In stating this, we are referring to learnings deeper than the lessons that we are taught from our parents—we are learning about who we are, who we are becoming, and who we want to be. While some parents encourage this type of learning, it is not true of all parents. Yet, the opportunity to learn through these changing relationships is ever-present—even after our parents are no longer living.

Few artists have explored the relationships with parents through their art with as much depth as Bruce Springsteen. During his 2016 "The River Tour," before singing "Independence Day," which was partially about his relationship with his father, he said about the song,

> It's the kind of song you write when you're young, and you're startled by your parents' humanity. You're shocked to find out that maybe they had their own dreams and their own desires and their own hopes that might not have panned out exactly as they had imagined. And you are at an age where all you can see are the adult compromises that they had to make, and you're still too young to understand and feel the blessings that come with compromise. So all you see is this small world that is closing in, closing in, closing in, and all you can think of is getting away from it. (March 31, 2016, Denver, Colorado)

Springsteen's idea of being startled by his parents' humanity is powerful. As children, we often do not see or experience our parents as fully human. We may not recognize that they have their own needs, their own hopes and dreams. Those moments when we begin to see our parents as fallible—and full—human beings can be painful and transformative. Regardless of whether you view your parents as good parents or not, this can be painful. But it also can be transformative and full of opportunity. We now have the opportunity to get to know our parents as human beings instead of idealized and/or villainized objects—human beings who have their gifts, and who have their flaws and limitations.

As is often the case, when the idealization breaks, there is sadness, frustration, and anger. But there also is opportunity to build a real, oftentimes deeper, relationship. These transitions vary across different cultural groups. In much of United States culture, we assume that rebellion and defiance is a necessary and universal part of growing up and separating from one's parents, especially for boys. However, this is not true with all cultures. At times, rebellion is associated with the privilege of being able to separate from one's family while, at other times, it is a product of the hyper-individualistic culture prominent in Euro-American culture.

As we grow older, each change in the relationship with our parents brings the need for grieving as well as the opportunity for deepening our relationship. We often grow from dependence upon our parents to reliance, from reliance to independence, from independence to our parents relying and eventually depending upon us. Through these changes we learn about our parents and about ourselves—if we are open to the lessons.

Being Parented as a Portal to Experience

Parents provide an essential context for children to begin exploring the world and their experience. John Bowlby (1969, 1973), the originator of attachment theory, supposed parent-child attachment provides a foundation for many aspects of development, including future relationships and one's sense of the world as a safe place. A secure attachment can provide a foundation for feeling safe to explore the world and one's own experience in the world.

Reflecting upon attachment, and how it impacted later relationships, can help understand how one experiences the world as an adult. Of course, many other factors, such as traumas, relationship ruptures, and cultural and religious experiences, also have an impact.

As a therapist, I (Louis) routinely ask in the first couple of sessions how emotion was expressed and reacted to in one's family growing up. This often sets an important tone for how emotions are viewed and experienced as an adult. When children are discouraged from expressing emotion or shamed for certain emotions, these emotions may become complicated later in life. Helping children recognize that emotions are normal and healthy is essential. While it is important for parents to help children learn to express their emotions in a healthy manner, the starting point for this is learning that it is okay to express emotions. As children grow older, they learn more effective ways to express these emotions and begin to learn where it is safe and not safe to express emotions. The starting point, however, is knowing that emotions are normal and healthy, and that it is okay to express them.

Similarly, children also learn from parents whether it is okay to explore new and different ideas. Parents tend to be invested in passing on their values to their children, and this can be a good thing. However, when this is done in an authoritarian manner that restricts the child in exploring different perspectives, this can be damaging. When children take on values from their parents in a rigid and authoritarian manner then these values often are not authentic in the child. They are experienced as an oppressive and often fear-based external system of rules instead of as authentic values. For many parents, balancing sharing one's values and encouraging exploration of new ideas is difficult. Parents may view exploring new ideas and values as a threat to their own meaning, to their authority, or to the relationship. When parents can tolerate their own fear and anxiety about this, then they are able to provide an important foundation for authenticity.

Parenting

Becoming a parent is a transformative experience. For many parents, they can never see the world the same way again. Will Smith (1997), in his song "Just the Two of Us," wrote about his experience of becoming a parent. He reflected upon the immediate changes when first being introduced to his son in the hospital, including fears of being enough and the rise of a protective instinct. The protective instinct manifested in taking an hour assuring that the car seat was in correctly and then getting angry at drivers who were driving too fast on the way home. Many parents can relate to the rise in anxiety and protectiveness, even if manifested in different expressions.

Maturing into the role of a parent involves reflecting upon what emerges in us during our adjustment to the role of parent. If one can remain open to what emerges, these varying emotional experiences provide an opportunity to learn and grow as a person and as a parent.

Parenting as a Portal to Self-Awareness

Becoming the best parent that we can be is an ongoing process that again requires us to learn about ourselves—and parenting provides many opportunities to do this. It is important to do more than learn parenting skills; we must learn about ourselves, who we are, and the values that guide our life.

***

Introduction

Shortly after I (Louis) graduated with my doctoral degree, I began teaching in a graduate psychology program. A good friend of mine, Brittany Garrett-Bowser, became a parent during this time. I remember sitting in her office one day as she said, "Parenting is some of the best therapy. You learn a lot about yourself and your parents when you become one." This really stayed with me, and I spent quite some time meditating on this. Although I cannot remember for sure if it was before or after this conversation with Brittany, one of the phrases I began using frequently when teaching—and at times with clients—was, "The best gift you can give your children is to be in therapy before you become a parent."

Years later, when I became a parent, Brittany's words returned to me often. I had been in therapy myself by this time—several times actually. I loved the process of being in therapy and exploring myself. I knew this prepared me to be a better parent, and I thought I knew myself pretty well by the time I became one. Yet, after my son was born, I found myself learning more and more. Some of the lessons were really more reinforcements of what I already knew, while other lessons took me by surprise. When my first child, Lakoda, was just a few months old, I started a routine when he would wake up at night. I would take him downstairs, grab his bottle, and talk to him. Often, I would share the values I hoped he would have as an adult. One of the first things I always told him was that I hoped he would treat women with respect. While I knew that was a value of mine, I was surprised that it was one of the first things that always came to mind. The second value that I would always share is that I hoped he would try to make the world a better place and value compassion and meaning more than money and even happiness. As I shared these hopes with my son, I reinforced these values in myself.

***

Parenting as a Portal to Experience

When you first hold your child in your arms your experience of the world shifts. This may involve terror as well as joy. Becoming a parent intensifies all of one's experiences. The poem "After She Tells You" begins with these poignant lines, "she dreams of killing herself /even the light from the lamp feels different." These words can jolt one into a different emotional space if one opens oneself to the experience the poet is writing about. Hearing these words may even transport one into a different emotional and psychological space.

Parenting is full of unknowns and unexpecteds. While we may try to guide our children, we also are often taken on an emotional journey that we did not expect and were not prepared for. This is the beauty and tragedy of parenting. While it is tempting to try to control the experience to protect ourselves, this inevitably fails. Yet, even if it were to succeed, it would dull the experience of parenthood. Genuine relationships take us into unknown and uncontrollable spaces, and it is here that we can experience the awe and sacredness of these relationships.

Existential Parenting
The idea of *existential parenting* may sound ominous to some, particularly given the common misunderstandings of the word *existential*. Popular understandings of the word existential often revolve around death and morbidity. While existential philosophers and psychologists do take seriously issues such as death and suffering, there is much more to it than this. We are rooting the idea of existential parenting in existential–humanistic psychology, which is sometimes considered the American school of existential psychology (see Hoffman, Serlin, & Rubin, 2019; Krug, 2019; Schneider, 2019a).

We understand existential parenting as centering around several themes including:
1. **Valuing relational presence and depth with our children**. Existential psychology views relationship as primary (Yalom, 1980). However, it is almost cliché to say that relationships are important. When existentialists talk about relationship, they are referring to a special type of relationship that includes relational depth, vulnerability, and being present with others. In parents, this strives to move beyond the hierarchical relationship with children while recognizing that this is a gradual process as children become older and are more able to make their own choices. It also encourages parents to not hide their vulnerabilities and humanness from their children.
2. **Empowering children toward making choices and taking responsibility**. Choice is an essential aspect of freedom, which is a core existential theme (May, 1981). Freedom, according to May, can only be understood in connection with limitation. Furthermore, as asserted by Frankl (1984), freedom can only be understood in the context of responsibility. Existential parenting encourages children early on to begin embracing their freedom while also recognizing how their choices are

connected to consequences. This approach to parenting values empowerment. By valuing the empowerment toward choice, parents gradually—in consideration of the individual child's development—relinquish their parental power and trust their child's ability to begin making choices. Through our relationship, we help our children understand the consequences of these choices (i.e., responsibility). This process allows children to come to experientially understand that with freedom and choice comes responsibility.

3. **Valuing empathy and compassion.** Empathy, from an existential perspective, is an experience in which we share in the emotional experience of others (Hoffman, 2019). Empathy is something we cultivate and embody, not something that we do. In other words, to develop empathy we work to remain open to the other person's experience and to taking this in to dwell inside of us as well. However, empathy is never perfect. It is vital that we recognize that we can never fully know or understand someone's experience through empathy, regardless of how empathetic we are. Compassion bears similarities to empathy but is more focused on acceptance and concern for all people in recognition of their human context, which includes the challenges and limitations they face. In existential parenting, we strive to teach our children empathy and compassion experientially—through our own empathy and compassion toward them. Through this experiential teaching, supplemented with helping them understand the importance of these values, we nurture our children to become compassionate, empathetic people.

4. **Valuing the spectrum of emotions.** From an existential perspective, all emotions, at their base, are healthy. They are not something to simply manage or control, but something that we strive to listen to and live with. In existential parenting, we strive to help our children become curious about their emotions and comfortable expressing them.

5. **Helping children explore their experiences.** Parents can play a vital role for children by guiding them in exploring their own experiences, which can include exploring their emotions. Yet, exploring experiences is broader and also includes thoughts, relationships, values, limitations, and other aspects of their humanness.

6. **Recognizing the importance of facing life directly and honestly.** This value is a difficult one for many parents. Our instinct is to protect our children from harm. While it is important to protect our children from many types of harm, this does not mean sheltering them from the world. Rather, we work to help children recognize the beauty and awe of existence as well as the challenges and limitations of life. This helps to prepare children for the real world. While this should be done gradually in consideration of the individual child's development and resources, many parents use the developmental argument of "they are not ready" to over-protect and shelter children. Balancing protection and facing life honestly is not easy and no parent does this perfectly; however, helping children to recognize our own limitations and imperfections is part of helping them to face life directly.
7. **Raising children to attend to meaning and purpose in life.** Frankl (1984) maintained that human beings are meaning-seeking creatures. Meaning in life is seen as a fundamental human need. While there can be many types of meaning in life, some types of meaning are more sustainable than others. Too often in contemporary culture, meaning gets lost in our priorities of making money, seeking power, and seeking recognition (see Vos, 2019). Money, power, and recognition tend to be shallow forms of meaning that do not sustain people. Existential parenting encourages children to seek out deeper, more sustaining forms of meaning such as relationships, making a contribution to the betterment of others and society, and fully embracing life. However, it also recognizes that meanings are personal and that ultimately it is more important to help children find their own meaning.
8. **Recognition of the uniqueness and connectedness of our children.** As with many existential values, uniqueness is paradoxical. While we help children understand how they are unique individuals and foster their individual development, it is important that we also help them to understand and appreciate that they are part of a culture, a family, and other identities that shape who they become. Existential psychologist James Bugental (1999) recognized this in connection with our paradoxical desires to be "a-part-of" and "apart from." If we focus only on helping our children recognize their uniqueness, we have failed them. If we emphasize their group identities

(family identity, cultural identity) to the neglect of their uniqueness, we do them a disservice. Existential parenting emphasizes the importance of recognizing the fullness of our children, which includes their uniqueness and connectedness.

9. **Recognition of the potential of our children.** The history of psychology too often focused primarily on the identification of pathology and problems. In the 1950s and 1960s, humanistic psychology began to form as an alternative to the mainstream perspectives that focused on deficits (Grogan, 2013). Instead, humanistic psychology advocated that we *also* must focus on human potential. However, existential–humanistic perspectives emphasize that we can only understand our potential in the context of our limitations (May, 1981; Yalom, 1980). Thus, existential parenting prioritizes empowering children to recognize and embrace their potential in the context of their limitations.

10. **Embracing Awe and Curiosity.** Kirk Schneider (2004, 2009, 2019b) has been writing about the transformative power of awe for a number of years, including the value of this for children. Awe brings us into touch with the unknown and unknowable with a sense of curiosity and wonder. Closely related to awe is curiosity. Awe and curiosity have a powerful transformative power; however, they are not easy to cultivate. They require vulnerability and humility. As an example, when individuals learn to become curious about their anxieties and fears, the power of these fears often is disarmed. The emotions do not necessarily go away and may not even change in intensity, yet one's experience of the emotion does change. Awe and curiosity embrace these anxieties. Existential parenting works to cultivate the experience of curiosity and awe in children. However, children often are much better at this than parents. Despite this, it is still important for parents to work to cultivate this in children. When children experience parents encouraging curiosity and awe, they are more likely to sustain these qualities as they get older. Too often, growing up results in losing these vital qualities. Existential parenting is committed to helping children retain these qualities in a manner that can be sustained through their lifespan.

Parenting After Trayvon Martin

We, the editors of this book and authors of this Introduction, are both parents of children of color. For us, it would be difficult and even inauthentic to write any book on parenting without considering the reality of raising children of color in our contemporary world. But we are not just constructing this book, or writing this section of the book, for parents of children of color; we are writing it with all parents in mind.

It is critical for parents of White children, too, to be aware of the realities of raising children of color. To move beyond the current reality of racial tension and violence, it is necessary for parents of children of color and White children alike to raise children who are socially conscious and committed to being anti-racist.

Trayvon Martin has become a powerful symbol in contemporary US culture. Although most are familiar with Trayvon's story, we will briefly revisit some of the details. On February 26, 2012, Trayvon Martin was walking back to his father's fiancé's house, where he was staying, after a trip to a convenience store. George Zimmerman, viewing him as suspicious, followed Trayvon with a gun and eventually confronted him. This led to a struggle between Trayvon and Zimmerman that resulted in Trayvon being shot and killed.

Trayvon's story is not unusual. People of color have long been familiar with being seen as suspicious and being attacked or even killed for these perceptions of them. Parents of children of color have long feared for the safety of their children in a world that views them through prejudiced eyes. Following Martin's death there were protests calling for a full investigation. Zimmerman was put on trial, and his lawyer used the "stand your ground" law as his defense. He later was found not guilty. The protests surrounding Trayvon's death led to the start of the Black Lives Matter movement that quickly became misunderstood as it was viewed through polarized lenses (see Hoffman et al., 2016).

It is important to emphasize, once again, that what happened to Trayvon is similar to what had happened previously to many people of color. But something changed with his death. The change came through the attention that the protests brought to this issue.

The poem "My Perfect, Imperfect Son" was written the day after the Zimmerman verdict. Many of the lines in this poem were drawn from comments that were made about Trayvon Martin. For example, the line "If you dress like that/You better be prepared to act accordingly," although not an exact quote, was drawn from a dialogue with someone that felt Trayvon Martin deserved what he got because of how he dressed. Too often, children of color are viewed as suspicious just for being.

Parents of children of color are thrown into many aspects of existential parenting. While the parents of many White children have the privilege of sheltering their children from some of the realities of the world, parents of children of color often have to take aspects of their children's innocence away to protect them. For example, many BIPOC (Black, Indigenous, People of Color) parents have to teach their children that if they play with guns in public spaces, they are more likely than White children to be perceived as dangerous and killed (i.e., Tamir Rice). BIPOC children have to learn that if they are with White friends and engage in what is often viewed as "typical adolescent fun," they are more likely to be criminalized and have consequences. BIPOC children have to learn that if they drive in a neighborhood that is predominantly White they may be viewed as being "out of place" or suspicious. BIPOC children need to be prepared for the racism that they may face in school from peers and even teachers, administrators, and other parents.

This is a harsh reality. But it is their reality. Many parents cannot relate to conversations about topics such as "When do we take our child's innocence away to protect them?" and "How do we teach our children to be prepared for racism without teaching them to fear White people?" These are painful, but necessary, conversations that occur regularly in the households where BIPOC children live.

While this may seem daunting and depressing, this is only part of raising BIPOC children. There are many gifts and opportunities as well. For example, we can raise children to be wise and prepared to face challenges of many varieties with integrity. We can raise children to recognize the beauty in those who are different from us. We can prepare our children to make a positive difference in the world and to be social justice advocates from a young age. We can raise our children to be compassionate toward those who suffer. We can raise our children to deeply know who they are as cultural beings and to deeply value their culture.

About this Book

Lullabies and Confessions is the eleventh book in the Poetry, Healing, and Growth Series. We, the editors, were inspired to conceive this book from our own reflections on parenting, including the blessings and challenges it has brought to our lives. Being a parent is a deep part of our identity.

The Poetry, Healing, and Growth series has prioritized healing poetry that is accessible. Our hope is that many will read these poems and be inspired to write their own poems. While each of the books in the Poetry, Healing, and Growth series include poets who have been published in literary journals and won awards, the books also include poets who have never been published before—and maybe never even shared a poem they have written with someone before. Most important, we wanted poems that would move people to feel and to reflect.

How to Use *Lullabies & Confessions*

There is no one correct way to use this book. We encourage people to find what works for them. You may want to read through this book slowly, or you may want to read through it all at once. You may want to read through the activities at the end of the book before you read the first poem. You may want to keep a journal nearby and write your own poems as you are inspired by poems that you read. We hope that you earmark some poems to return to over and over, and that you underline lines that evoked emotions or maybe just curiosity or even confusion. In other words, we hope you engage with this book.

We offer this book with hopes that it will be a useful book, not just a book designed for the pleasure of reading poetry. Our hope, more than anything, is that this book will lead you into reflection. And that you may find inspiration to write your own poems—without concern about the quality of the poems or how others may respond to your poetry. When writing poems for healing and growth, apprehension about the quality of the poem is a distraction from its possibilities and potentialities. Whether the poem is an artistic masterpiece or just your own explorations of your feelings and thoughts, the poem can be healing and growth facilitating. Certainly, not all the poems in this collection, including our own, are masterpieces. Yet, they are contributions we believe have the potential to evoke something in the readers that will be of value to them.

Conclusion

We are grateful that you decided our book is worth the time investment. Many of the poems on the pages ahead emerged from places of deep angst and reflection. Others emerged from the joyous experience of one's relationship with their child or parent. These poems reflect a wide range of parent–child experiences that illuminate the human condition. If you open yourself to them, they just may inspire you to connect more deeply with the awe and wonderment of life and relationship.

As you read through these poems, we hope you will allow them to take you on a journey into new and unexpected places!

References

Bowlby, J. (1969). *Attachment and loss* (Vol. 1: Attachment). Basic Books.

Bowlby, J. (1973). *Attachment and loss.* (Vol. 2: Separation). Basic Books.

Bugental, J. F. T. (1999). *Psychotherapy isn't what you think.* Zeig, Tucker, & Co.

Frankl, V. E. (1984). *Man's search for meaning: An introduction to Logotherapy* (3rd ed.). Simon & Schuster.

Hoffman, L. (2019). Culture and empathy in humanistic psychology. In L. Hoffman, H. P. Cleare-Hoffman, N. Granger, Jr., & D. St. John (Eds.), *Humanistic approaches to multiculturalism and diversity: Perspectives on existence and difference* (pp. 103–116). Routledge.

Hoffman, L., Granger, N. Jr., Vallejos, L., & Moats, M. (2016). An existential–humanistic perspective on Black Lives Matter and contemporary protest movements. *Journal of Humanistic Psychology, 56,* 595–611. https://doi.org/10.1177/0022167816652273

Hoffman, L., Serlin, I. D., & Rubin, S. (2019). The history of existential–humanistic and existential-integrative therapy. In. E. van Duerzen, E. Craig, A. Längle, K. J. Schneider, D. Tantam, & S. du Plock (Eds.), *The Wiley world handbook of existential therapy* (pp. 235–246). Wiley.

Krug, O. T. (2019). Existential–humanistic and existential–integrative therapy: Philosophy and theory. In. E. van Duerzen, E. Craig, A. Längle, K. J. Schneider, D. Tantam, & S. du Plock (Eds.), *The Wiley world handbook of existential therapy* (pp. 247–256). Wiley.

May, R. (1981). *Freedom and destiny.* Norton.

Schneider, K. J. (2004). *Rediscovery of awe: Splendor, mystery, and the fluid center of life.* Paragon House.

Schneider, K. J. (2009). *Awakening to awe: Personal stories of profound transformation.* Jason Aronson.

Schneider, K. J. (2019a). Existential–humanistic and existential–integrative therapy: Method and practice. In. E. van Duerzen, E. Craig, A. Längle, K. J. Schneider, D. Tantam, & S. du Plock (Eds.), *The Wiley world handbook of existential therapy* (pp. 257–266). Wiley.

Schneider, K. J. (2019b). *The spirituality of awe: Challenges to the robotic revolution* (rev. ed.). University Professors Press.

Smith, W. (1997). Just the two of us. On *Big Willie Style* [CD]. Columbia

Records.
Vos, J. (2019). *The economics of meaning in life: From capitalist life syndrome to meaning-oriented economies.* University Professors Press.
Yalom, I. D. (1980). *Existential psychotherapy.* Basic Books.

Poems

The Light Inside
Alan King

for Jazmyn King

You were a print of light pressed
into a waxy dark sheet. Your mom framed you
while I carried you in my wallet and phone.

I stood in your white room — the black window
trim and floor boards, the Espresso dresser and
crib watched me fold your onesies,

watched me contemplate the country of fatherhood,
where experience alone won't grant you citizenship.

I hang the fluffy pink sleepsack, the doll-like plaid
dress, the white coverall and cap freckled with
green and blue cockatoos.

Everything hangs, waiting for you to fill them
the way your mom and I waited for you

to fill her womb, we waited through the tears —
pacing and praying you'd be stronger than the ones before,
barely a glimmer when they dimmed.

Now, your mom's a lamp, whose light comes
from your kicks and punches, from watching the star
in your chest flash on the ultrasound,
from your persistence to enter our life.

If there's one thing waiting taught us
it's that patience is the currency
of anything worth having.

So I rub your mom's tummy to
feel your elbow, then your fist —
grateful for the light inside.

Icarus's Mother Talks to Her Son
Lois Marie Harrod

I was not given your father's
        engineering mind

and the harpies refuse to bear
        me up.

So I act a life and sometimes live
        it unconsciously

a moment now and now,
        but then

my son, you are thirty-five and still jumping
        off garage roofs as you did at five,

down-shattering your foot bones
        and hobbling

for hours pretending your shoes
        don't hurt

as if to prove the body has its reasons
        which the brain

can stand — these manic highs of yours,
        these madman wings

that inevitably melt down their wax
        to solitude,

the ocean you so blithely flew as a teenager
        a weedy millpond

and the great sun
        a star so far gone

no one can touch it
> with the most sensitive telescope.

Who can reach you — and what
> does the oracle say?

Years we have been moving apart
> and you never held

flights of conversation worth preserving —
> feather-soothing, louse-plucking

gnat-clouding — and the self?
> one more two-winged construct,

what's the point?
> Don't you know I know

my briefest hug offends you.
> You want me far away,

I want you to take
> your medications

so that you can be a little more kin
> and kind and I can say

I've been there, my child, I am there
> now in that self-concerned pond

that flows nowhere, I too tried to fly
> in my own grave

way and I still love you, child,
> as I loved you as a child,

floating or falling,
> whatever flying means.

***

"Icarus's Mother Talks to Her Son" was originally published in *Weber: The Contemporary West.*

Mother by Any Means
Ellaraine Lockie

She's sitting on my bar stool
when I come back from the bathroom
Her hand clamping a cocktail napkin
over my cream sherry
Don't I know there are men
who drug women's drinks?

She glares across the table
above cups of green tea
Concerned over a man I've met online
A masterful poet who metered
murdering half the population of L.A.
A maniac she admonishes
And don't mail him your address

She's pacing the New Mexican
motel room at midnight
when I return from the grocery store
Where locally grown produce
overpowered me for an extra hour
She's unable to understand
the epicurean pull of sixteen species
of peppers with recipes honoring each
I'm unable to understand her panic
that I was impounded by something
more menacing than a pepper

Until I remember motherhood
when she was an adolescent
and saw herself immortal
Contrary to me now
who knows I could die any day
I elect not to allude to the
charging rhino in South Africa
Nor mention the motorcycle and marijuana
I'm saving for special occasions
Omissions kindred no doubt

to my daughter's when I waited up late
for the end of each date

***

"Mother by Any Means" was originally published in *Chiron Review* (2004). Republished with permission.

Not My Mother's Daughter
Lisa Xochitl Vallejos

Act I

She climbed a tree as a child
To escape the torment of elder siblings
That used the younger as targets
For their own aggression
She climbed to escape the punishment
Of an electrical cord
Wielded by a harried mother
Wrangling 9 children on her own
Who sopped up the bean juice
With a small tortilla and called
It a meal
She climbed that tree to escape the
Laughs, sneers, and pointed whispers
Of a childless father
Whose daddy was alive and well
Lost in a bottle of cheap liquor

Act II

Even as a young girl
I felt her absence although
She was there
In the smile that never reached her eyes
A laugh that seemed forced
How she never really saw me
Even when I was *rightthereinherface*
I wanted to be enough
I wanted to be loved
But you can't love a child when your
Heart is in a tree
The song lyrics that penetrated my childhood
Haunted me
Taunted me and I feared that
"maybe I'm just like my mother—she's never satisfied"
When feeling broken became too much

I followed her lead
And left my heart somewhere safe

Act III

He burst into this world from my womb
Pulling my heart out of its hiding place
Where he held it solidly in his tiny palm
Until his sister came and took her share
Together, they captivated me
Weaving their little beings into every fiber
Of my essence
Reaching for my hand and gripping my soul
And my god, mothering can hurt sometimes
Sharing their pain cuts to my marrow
The love I feel ravages me completely
I am as one without skin, raw and exposed
Able to be destroyed because love
Has made me vulnerable

Act IV

Now as tender as the babes I birthed
Life's vicissitudes leaving scars
As evidence of living well
I hold them both in good times
Challenging times
I have learned to love the girl I was
I love the girl still trapped in a tree
As I hold all of us closely in my wide-open heart
I catch a glimpse of the woman I have become
And smile as I see
I am not my mother's daughter.

Every Version
Louis Hoffman

For Lakoda, Lukaya, and Lyon

I wish I could write a perfect poem
for each age
or even one
just good enough
to remember you by
I'd make us a book
of poems and photos
so that I could remember....

That infectious laugh
I had to capture
each time I left town
The sweet curled up snuggles
I looked forward to
each night on the couch
The age where you followed me everywhere
yelling "Ouis! Ouis!"
when you could not find me
That trip across country
—just the two of us
when you ran down that rock
Terrified, I could just watch
Our trip to Yosemite
and visit to the tea house
where you seemed such a little man
Our visits to the zoo
where, to your delight, we visited the lions
again and again and again

Each new phase
I celebrated the new you
eagerly meeting the changes
and struggling to let go
of the you I once knew

Each day I grieve the you
that fades into memories

Some days I want to tell you
about the paradox
the loving...
the meeting...
the letting go...
the grieving...
all weaved together
A tapestry of different yous
But I wait
Knowing you could not yet understand

I have loved every version
of you

By What Right?
Tom Greening

By what right, or luck,
have I lived over a decade longer
than my father did?
He did not smoke,
rarely drank alcohol,
ate well, exercised,
attended church,
retired at 70,
died at 73.
Walking on the beach,
breathing New England air,
singing hymns,
were not enough
to beat cancer.
Now he's been gone
almost half a century,
and my own time
is running out.
Can he still guide me?

Fear of Heights
Carol Barrett

I had forgotten my father
built me stilts, cedar poles polished
like a hope chest, foot-ledge secured
by a strip of tire. Forgotten
how I clamored over the lawn
like a heron with broken leg,
the driveway too unforgiving
for spills, my hands flailing the air,
the smell of clover on landing,
steady coaching: try it again.

Somebody mentioned stilts and I
fell back to that place – we are called
to account for things – persistent
mole hills, border geraniums
bitter as daisies even now.
I think of wood, of how my breath
leapt out of its cage the first time
I drove across a narrow bridge
on the Mississippi, alone,
without knowing what lay ahead,
what skies or ground or red flowers
blooming. My father loved me well.

He thought I could do anything,
boy, or girl, the child who came
lumbering along, heaven-sent
after my mother's miscarriage.
To think such legacy would drive
despair or elevate chagrin
to dread. Imagine that! I fell

and fell again, like a body
dropped from its lair of womb and still

the grain's in my hands, the wooden
dreaming, blood-born, propelled without
a conscious thought. He stopped me once,
released his hold: *I said you could
do anything, not everything.*

***

"Fear of Heights" was originally published in *Poetry Norwest, XLI*(3), 43. Republished with permission.

The Day She Stopped Telling Me Everything
Maura Snell

It wasn't so much the text messages
    or the pictures attached
that alerted me to this new era in our existence—
    the ones from my friend Laura
who had gone to the middle school talent show—
    but more the way my daughter responded
when I called to congratulate her on winning
    the whole damn thing
and she didn't even pick up her phone.
    It occurred to me
that the day she stopped telling me everything
    had already come and gone
like the popcorn guy at a Red Sox game,
    or the collection basket at Sunday services:
you have to really pay attention or it goes right by
    and then, you're left sitting there
on the edge of your seat with five dollars
    clutched in your fist.

I Hold a Small Death...
Christina Lovin

I hold a small death in my hands: blue
and pale, shape of a weeks-old
infant, stiff without cry or suck.

Lift it by the heels.

My body opened again: blood pulsed
between us then; now breath,
our lengthened cord.

Daughter I've borne twice: offspring
of my belly, live birth of my lungs.

***

"I Hold a Small Death..."was originally published in *God of Sparrows* (Delphi Series IX, Blue Lyra Press, 2020).

Bitties Turning 4
Marion Deutsche Cohen

"And YOU'RE getting bigger, too, Ma."
"No, I'm not getting bigger. I stopped growing a long time
    ago. Adults don't grow. Only kids grow."
"No, you're getting bigger."
"Oh, I see. YOU want me to keep getting bigger so that way, when you
   get bigger, I'll still be big, to you."
"Yeah."
And then he probably starts sucking his thumb.
And I probably say "Come on over here, Lovey."
And maybe he starts eating on me.
Or maybe he just runs off to play with some toy.

Right Field Siberia
Charlotte Mandel

If his arms didn't hang
like dead eels in oversized
little league sleeves
dangling from shoulders
compressed by the weight of
the whole town's name on his back

then my chest wouldn't hurt
as I shiver in raw
spring season
braced against wind
like a fisherman's rasp
scaling my skin,
a woman in sandals,
praying for an out, already, a final
out.

He's light on his feet
could run if ever
he hit a ball
could throw if ever
he stopped one in the air.
Everybody knows right field's
the Siberian slot—not even
a lefthanded nine-year-old
bats it to there.

Two fathers next to me
smoke and grin and cheer—
the score is 26 to 23—
27 now—I think we're ahead
watching four or five
crack-run-fumble-bases-loaded innings.

Oh, son, wave your chilblained hands,
peel off that duckbill and run—
forgive us and come

with your Dad to his lab, to me in my studio
between us there wasn't a single
athletic gene to send
sliding into your blood's home base.

***

"Right Field Siberia" was originally published in *Your Daily Poem* (online, 4/5/13). Republished with permission.

The Genes of Guilt
Patricia Wellingham-Jones

The only wrinkled forehead in the whole
first grade picture, my father looks
off to the side with a responsible frown,
the gathering glance
of trouble on the way
he wore for his long helping life.
I wonder
caught in the blood
bond of caring
how many generations have transmitted
that particular gene
to the eldest child afflicted
with the admonition
take care of your sister
and
at what point in two aging
lives one can simply let go
to let the other
live without rescue
from the almost empty
pantry of plenty
or
do they go to their separate graves
fingers outstretched
reluctant drops doled
and
if the sequence breaks
can the one stumble
without the other shattering in guilt?
I wonder
how many generations
passed on that frown
to the little face in the faded photo.

***

"The Genes of Guilt" was originally published in *millers pond* (2002). Reprinted with permission.

Why I Chose My Parents
Shoshauna Shy

Although I liked the way he chided her,
I wasn't convinced.
So I loitered in their little Illinois kitchen
with its terrycloth toaster cover and silk-
screened curtain, watched them eat
Kellogg's Corn Flakes, bananas
under dollops of sour cream,
Push-Ups on hot days. She did pliés while
listening to the radio; he sat in the breezeway
sketching with charcoal.

I had started following them at a camp banquet
where he first saw her jitterbugging with
another guy, then tossed twigs at a friend's
cleavage to make her jealous, way before they
ran into each other on a streetcar, way before
she decided he wasn't such a jerk, after all,
and packed tuna fish sandwiches for their
bike ride to Euclid Creek.
Had my eye on a couple in Cincinnati too

although next thing I knew, my mom & dad
were posing for a photo, their firstborn son
barely old enough to walk dressed in saddle shoes
and seated plumb between them.

He had a smile wider than Nebraska.
That clinched it for me.

***

"Why I Chose My Parents" was originally published in *The Splash of Easy Laughter* by Shoshauna Shy (Kelsay Books, 2017). Republished with permission.

Ice Storm
W. F. Lantry

Wind in the summer trees: the rising air
carries a goshawk near dark thunderstorms.
He glides, backlit, highlighted in this glare:
effortless wings track where the updraft warms.
But we, here far below, struggle to tread
through fallen branches, brambles, thorned rose canes
grasping our legs and arms. The forest seems
a maze of fallen trunks. A blizzard spread
destruction through this woodland. What remains
blocks our old paths, and redirects the streams.

The snow began at dawn. Lovely and cold
it fell, and kept on falling. Its precise
layers became a garment to enfold
the house and us in one thick robe of ice.
Then wind came up at noon. Our power died.
The cold infected everything. We talked,
wrapped in our blankets, of some quick escape
but knew the truth, knew, freezing, we'd decide
to leave. The snow blew past her as she walked,
and darkening, obscured her moving shape.

An hour later, we began to dress,
young James and Daniel put on boots, then wrapped
wool scarves across their faces. My endless
cajoling reassured them we weren't trapped,
until we went outside: the drifting snow
at four feet, towered over brave young James,
and even Daniel, shouldering into
his role as lead, began to falter, slow
and stop. The daylight flickered. Broken frames
of cherry branches blocked us, and we knew

we needed help. We'd gone five hundred feet,
the road was half a mile away. The dark
was gathering. Its wind promised defeat
here, in this foreign place, frozen and stark.

We tried to push ahead. And then we saw
through halfdusk, Julian, who'd doubled back,
worried we hadn't come. He cleared away
the obstacles, and pulled James through a draw
between the rising drifts. He took my pack
and led us out, just at the fall of day.

Distant headlights beacons: Julian's words
cajoled his brother, one last time, to lift
himself back up. Silence. No singing birds,
their mother's voice this blizzard's only gift.
We found her warmth, and fled. Since then, the wind
has taken on new meaning. Every breeze
even this summer's storm, recalls that walk
through icy woods, and trembling, I begin
negotiating pathways through these trees
guided by lost cries of an unseen hawk.

Night Fear
Charles Rossiter

Three a.m., he wakes
and calls for a hold
so I go and hold him.
He says he's scared.

I tell him to look at books
or recite the presidents.
3:55 he calls again
and there are real tears.
He says it's nothing specific,
he's just scared.

I hold him again and repeat
the book idea. This time
he says *ok, give me books*
I pile some on his bed
and say *sweet dreams.*

For a while I hear
the pages turning
and his five and a half
year old voice
as I drift
between wake and sleep.

At 5:15 he comes over
again. This time
I don't push him on it.
I know what he's afraid of.
I throw the covers back
and let him in.

***

"Night Fear" was previously published in *the Journal of Poetry Therapy.* Republished with permission.

Definition
Marilyn Zelke Windau

I am a box of time.
Open now I flow upwards,
outwards.
I meander through books
in the forbidden cabinet of childhood.
I see the ballerina poses
in the smallest brown leather
volume on the shelf.
I tour jeté through many seasons in footlights.
Three girls, my daughters,
now share my air flow currents.
Rising we are
dancing the breezes of life.

***

"Definition" was previously published in *Owning Shadows* by Marilyn Zelke Windau (Kelsay Books, 2017). Republished with permission.

The Hundred Names of Love
Annie Lighthart

The children have gone to bed.
We are so tired we could fold ourselves neatly
behind our eyes and sleep mid-word, sleep standing
warm among the creatures in the barn, lean together
and sleep, forgetting each other completely in the velvet,
the forgiveness of that sleep.

Then the one small cry:
one strike of the match-head of sound:
one child's voice:
and the hundred names of love are lit
as we rise and walk down the hall.

One hundred nights we wake like this,
wake out of our nowhere
to kneel by small beds in darkness.
One hundred flowers open in our hands,
a name for love written in each one.

***

"The Hundred Names of Love" was originally published in *Iron String* (Airlie Press, 2013). Reprinted with permission.

I Go Back in Time and Rescue My Mother
Leah Browning

I know just where to find her, standing at the stove,
frying potato latkes in a cast-iron skillet. Her apron
is spattered with dark spots of grease, and waves
of heat rise up from the stove, pasting her dark hair
against the dampness of her neck and temples.

"Can't you make them any faster?" I am asking,
ten years old, at the table with my brother and sister.
The little pancakes are made of raw potato, grated
into a bowl and mixed with egg and salt and pepper.

It is dark outside, early winter. I arrive as a gust
of cold air, blowing in under the front door, hovering
in the space over the table, over the serving plate
with its bed of paper towels to absorb the excess oil.

There have been so many times that she's said,
"I just want to run away," spoken in anger
and in desperation, that I expect her to come
willingly, to take the ghostly fingers I offer
and allow herself to be pulled away

from all of us, from that life—the whining,
bickering children, the unfulfilled ambitions,
the husband who works long hours and listens
from a distance. The loneliness. The emptiness.

Everything that I know now she must have felt.
"I can save you," I whisper, pulling at her hand,
but she slips away, turning instead toward the table,
squandering what feels like her only chance for escape,

though the door is unlocked and she's chosen a million
times to stay. So I seep out of my childhood
home and go back to my own life. To the whining,
bickering children, the unfulfilled ambitions,

the husband who works long hours and listens

from a distance. The loneliness. The emptiness.
My mother calls on weekends after going
to bookstores or concerts, after sleeping until ten.
I stand at the stove, cooking hot foods over cast iron.

When my daughter arrives from her future life
to save us both, I find that I scarcely feel the hint
of air on my hand. But I am ready. I've been waiting
years now for someone to come and rescue me.

She pulls my arm away from the clothes I am folding,
from the dirty dishes and the trash that needs to go out.
And we get all the way to the front door before I hear
her voice—nine and a half years old, siren sweet rising
up the stairs—and find that I, too, am unable to leave.

***

"I Go Back in Time and Rescue My Mother" was originally published in *Salome Magazine*, May 28, 2007, www.salomemagazine.com. Republished with permission.

"I Go Back in Time and Rescue My Mother" was previously published in *Family Pictures: Poems & Photographs Celebrating Our Loved Ones* edited by Kwame Alexander (Capital Bookfest, 2007). Republished with permission.

"I Go Back in Time and Rescue My Mother" was previously published in *Picking Cherries in the Española Valley* by Leah Browning (Dancing Girl Press, 2010). Republished with permission.

"I Go Back in Time and Rescue My Mother" was previously published in *Mamas and Papas: On the Sublime and Heartbreaking Art of Parenting* edited by Alys Masek and Kelly Mayhew (City Works Press, 2010). Republished with permission.

She's Moved to the Other Side of the World
Phyllis Wax

My mother has come to visit and I realize I don't know her. She doesn't speak much and her face has become expressionless. Her forehead is smooth but her eyes have shrunk into skin stretched so much it sags and hangs from the bones of her brow and cheeks.

She's shorter than she used to be and takes very small steps, as though she is restricted by a tight kimono. She's become traditional Japanese. But I don't know how to speak Japanese. I find myself bowing slightly and saying *ah so*. I half expect to hear her revert to Yiddish, the long ago language of secrets between her and my father. Maybe now I'll understand.

A Family Affair
Carol Barrett

Candles burned when the women made Lindon
upstairs, an attic loft with round windows.
The juice came in a clean jar of Grey Poupon,
half teaspoonful sucked into a glass
eye dropper. Molly made the first squeeze.
Marsha took it inside, cervix
pink and waiting. They met him
in a health food store, pleased
with his bicycler's body. He likes
lavender, and won't charge.
The clinic rate is a hundred dollars,
an hour old. No candles.

Just an idea once, Lindon
now wakes up each night. Runny nose,
he splats his tiny hands on the television,
smearing the six o'clock news.
Grandmother won't hear half
his story. She invents her own:
a deserting husband, too young
to be a proper father.
Better that, than friends
think her daughter did it
unmarried. Ashamed to learn so late
of the wedding, they send glass
doves and swans, while Marsha picks
a new family name.

Lindon does alright: furtive aunts
wait their turns, assuring him
Daddy certainly was a handsome man,
all that fine blond hair, strong thighs.
They would strangle Daddy if they could, prefer
to think him dead already, spare Marsha
painful details. As indulgent uncles
talk to Lindon's toes, they marvel
at how well she looks, not even showing

grief.

Candles burned when the women made Lindon.
In an attic loft with round windows
a little mustard goes a long way.

***

"A Family Affair" was originally published in *Conditions, 11/12*, 11-12, 1984. Reprinted with permission.

Going to Meet Our Birth Daughter After Nineteen Years
Maura Snell

We hold hands the whole way there.
        You steer with your left palm and knee

over roads old and familiar, through canyons,
        shifting mountain shadows   dust   rain.

We've been coming towards this
        for seven thousand days.
I've counted them all.

Once, I dreamt of a little girl in the back seat,

        buckled in tight, blonde tendrils
flying. Pink lips.   Laughter.

Almost there. You stop the car
so I can step out   catch my breath.

Gravel by the road fills my sandals.
When I shake out stones, one is turquoise.

        I slide it into my pocket.

I wonder
        if she will have freckles.

I already know she has your eyes.

I Want to be Ready
Louis Hoffman

For my mother

Mama, hold on
I want to be ready
For that day
For your dark embrace
To that comforting place
Far away from the pain of now
We've come far
But are not there yet
There are words
Still hidden
Memories unborn
Grandsons, too, needing memories
More than pictures

Mama, grant me
This one selfish desire
That you alone
Would bear the pain
Let me be ready...
Suffer this for me
And when you reach your solace
Beg for my forgiveness
For this merciless wish

***

"I Want to Be Ready" was originally published in *Capturing Shadows: Poetic Encounters Along the Path of Grief and Loss* by Louis Hoffman & Michael Moats (University Professors Press, 2015). Republished with permission.

I Never Called Him Foster
Nathaniel Granger, Jr.

Department of Human Services
Would just drop 'em off
Some would trade 'em
Some would misuse 'em
Some would hate 'em, even

"You know what your problem is?"
Over a score ago
Case manager once told
"You love these kids too much
And you are never supposed
To love them."

But Zack we loved
Sure, he didn't look like the others
He was White
And yes, he cut up, acted out
And did what teenagers do

He was the oldest
Older than my three
We would go places
And he was introduced as that—
My oldest son
I never called him "foster"

I grabbed him once by the shirt
It was the back of the mall
Security had called
A pair of earrings
Stolen for a girl at school

"You're not supposed to put hands on us"
Zack reminded me
I'm your Dad—
I'd rather go to jail for putting my hands on you
Than to see you go to jail for stealing.

Zack emancipated
Life traveled on
My kids are adults now
And, I'm more than a score older

Lying in bed
Home from the hospital
The phone rings
I refuse to talk to anyone
The phone rings, again,
And, again it rings…

Hello
"Hello, Dad?"
Who is this?
"This is Zack, your son.
Is this Dad?"

He shared his story
Twenty years' worth
"I had to find you.
My baby was born—
It brought back all the love you showed me."

I cried
He's alive
And, he is well; it is well
He still calls me Dad
I never called him "foster."

The Catch
W. F. Lantry

Spectacular, this February day,
both clear and warm, untroubled as we drive
the river parkway towards a concert hall
where hexagons are everywhere: they frame
both chandeliers and fixtures on the wall,
their forms repeating as we three arrive —
Kate, James, and I, climbing the steps as one

up to the balcony. James wants to run.
Why not? He's only seven. But the stares
of ushers calm him. When we find our seats
he's still a little bouncy. There's a game
he likes to play: he quietly repeats
my warnings: "'It's a long way down.' Who cares?"
I do. But could I catch him if he slipped?

I think back twenty years. One day, I gripped
my first-born's ankles tightly as he rode
my shoulders to the curbside mailbox.
That day, he bucked and twisted in the same
swift movement, started falling towards the rocks
headfirst behind me. Turning, as time slowed,
and reaching down, I barely caught the cuff

of one pant leg. The memory's enough
to make me anxious, even now. But soon
James settles back, attentive to the loud
conductor's introduction, hears his name
repeated, and begins to scan the crowd
for other children, as musicians tune
their instruments and lean forward to play.

At Jack London State Historic Park
Shahé Mankerian

Deep in the woods of Sonoma County, my daughter
and I stand under a eucalyptus tree. She's pensive

because she doesn't understand my adoration
of Dostoyevsky. "I wish you wrote like Jack London,"

she denounces. "Dostoyevsky didn't have dogs
like London. He didn't have the Pig Palace.

He didn't use a Remington Noiseless typewriter.
Dostoyevsky's Siberia doesn't compare to the ruins

of London's ill-fated Wolf House. Jack kissed Charmian
in the Valley of the Moon. Dostoyevsky had seizures.

Jack compared death to the last mosquito you
and I squashed. Dostoyevsky quoted Jesus when he died."

The Matter of Smiles
Marion Deutsche Cohen

after reading "The Magic Years"

(1)
The nurse hands him to me and smiles
I smile back
she smiles back-back.
And his face swivels between hers and mine
and decides to complete the triangle.
It's only a split but anyone could see:
That there exists more than one face
is to him AMUSING
and he, not exactly smiles
not exactly smirks
but something
something nice.

(2)
At six days, honest
on the big bed that twilight
Arin and I pass him back and back
and he recognizes it, the eternal triangle
and he does it again
only this time not a smirk
and not reflex
not gas
not even something.

(3)
Like a blind person's hand, and just as eager
his eyes are tracing our faces.
Left to right, he reads us
top to bottom.
Just as tender.
Just as slow.
But he doesn't have to go to the end
has already learned the context.
He remembers from trimesters ago
when, slowly in the dark, his own features were lighting up.

Yes, he recognizes us
in his image.
And he forms the smile
in our image.

***

"The Matter of Smiles" was previously published in *The Fuss and the Fury* by Marion Deutsche Cohon (Alien Buddha Press, 2019). Republished with permission.

My Window
Evgeny Krayushkin–ZheKa

I am the wall
And you—my window.
I sneak a gaze
And see
A better world—
In you.
You are the depth
Into a better me.

Learning from The Landscape
   (after Henri met de Bles)
Carol Dorf

It's a lucky girl who can look at this painting
of the city burning red into the black night
with its title "Landscape with Lot and His Daughters,"
without reflecting on her father, and what he taught
her about being a girl turned woman, or male
power and mobs, how the angels were all too ready
to interfere in everyone's lives. This town
is set on a lake, yet there are no fireboats
visible to do something about the conflagration.
Lot's daughters and his wife go unnamed
in the biblical version. In another version, Ado,
wife and mother, can't bear to say goodbye
to her city, all the neighbors, her own mother
and becomes frozen by loss, while her daughters
Pheiné and *Thamma* travel with the drunken
father until they run off with their own children,
never looking back while he dozes off
another binge. Only here does the bear
enter the story, territorial with new cubs.

Two Balloons
Michael Moats

Today, I stared at a bunch of balloons
Blue and gold, blue and gold, blue and gold
All grouped together and pressing against the ceiling.

I spotted two in the crowd
One gold and one blue
And they were special.

With a feeling of sadness and a need for privacy
I left the house full of people,
Holding my two balloons.

The breeze was warm and light.
The pines had covered everything
In their shower of pollen.

I gaze at each of the balloons.
Their faces become clearer,
My chest becomes heavy.

Quietly I speak,
"I wish you the best, and it is time to let go."
There is a brief pause before releasing my grasp.

Still wanting to help
I gently raise my hand
As if to give the balloons an unnecessary lift.

The strings glide across my palm
As they begin their ascent.
Sadness and excitement combine.

My golden balloon respectfully and slowly began,
Until the string left my hand
And then she soared.

Direct and purposeful
She cleared the light currents

To enter the turmoil and openness that would propel her.

I watch her as my blue balloon seems to linger.
My eyes switching back and forth,
Capturing as much as I can of each.

Blue boy seems to be ready to go
But not in a hurry.
There is comfort in what is familiar.

He clings close to the towering pine
That has shielded him, yet
Careful not to attach to its projecting branches.

Almost as if he is looking around
And testing the winds for direction,
He clears the shroud of protection and goes.

A golden shimmer is almost invisible,
Invisible in the vast blue sky.
Yet, she continues to rise.

Seconds pass,
And I am left alone
With my symbolism.

Silent, sad, smiling, excited.
Reflections and dreams.
Be well, my kids.

***

"Two Balloons" was originally published in *Capturing Shadows: Poetic Encounters Along the Path of Grief and Loss* by Louis Hoffman & Michael Moats (University Professors Press, 2015). Republished with permission.

Empty Nest
Michele Riedel

What speaks to me are the long silences of open doors that
once carried the melody of your voice in its creaking opening/closing
and your singing that brushed the hallway walls with hues of liquid
 yellows.
My heart in tune with your smiling eyes and living rhythm.
Strong willow — best be gone to test your branches.
Bending fro and back in youthfulness as you ride the waves of life's
 choices.

A Mother is Gathering Pens...
Marilyn Flower

A mother is gathering pens
to grade her students' essays
when a knife tears open her heart.
She feels her son lost in the forest,
phones him across the country.
A voicemail, darkness—he is not there.
Runes told at a party
spoke this terrible absence:
"He needs space to fall and get
up by himself."

Her cat settles against her,
comfort warm and deep
yet pain spreads
to the small bones of her back.
She dreams of a field,
vast with ancient growth–
towering thistles, life-stripped trees..
When she wakes, her son
is in the next room, arguing,
gesturing to his father,
perhaps safe.

Mother and Son
Nesreen Frost

I hovered
Smothered your plump cheeks
With kisses
And attended
To your needs
Now
I care
I protect
and
I teach

Ancient wisdom and love travels through my blood
Guided me and held me up

I discovered
a whole new world
of hurt when you hurt
But I smile to preserve
a sense of security
Take a deep breath
Take a big step
on clouds of air
On softly cushioned stairs

What started as a show for you
turned into a habit within
Dark tornadoes
And strong winds
still exist
Amidst the bright sun
that drizzles in

This tropical drift
Tamed by my pen
Filtered through my lens
Worked out the kinks
in my own time and space

I came to you with traces
of the wounds
Glimpses of the places
you may travel
Showed you I am human too
And that you
don't have to break
in the face
of adversity
Don't have to lose your integrity
Don't have to ignore the heart
That is giving you life
Maybe you can
Study its beats
Learn from its leaks
Bend when it needs
Make it your friend
And try to transcend
the temporary states
You can make your mistakes
Result in growth

My boys
My little seeds
Once kept warm
In my arms
A part of you
I will always hold
In pure love and light

You are becoming your own men
Soul lending you strength
Your minds taking flight
Making your own decisions
And finding your positions
Eagerly and respectfully
In this world
You will be
Spreading out
Soon
But never lost

Zoe Dances
Milton J. Bates

Watching her spin across
the kitchen floor, arms extended
left and right for balance,
we wonder how we'd missed it:
our granddaughter is destined
to be a prima ballerina.

Last week, observing how
she tracked a column of red ants
up a sycamore, we were sure
she would become a naturalist.

The week before, she was
another Julia Child,
stirring in her saucepan
an imaginary Béarnaise.

What did our grown-ups foresee
for us at fifteen months?
Bruised from bumping against
the ceiling of early promise,
they needed to believe
in our limitless potential.

We wear those bruises too,
so we draw no conclusions
when Zoe lands dizzy
and diaper-bottomed on the floor.

Swedish Rye

Christina Lovin

What is it that I fear to smear like grease
across the starched white apron
of this page? Memories that cling and prick
like caraway between the teeth:

my father singing in the kitchen
as he kneaded dark rye dough
across a wooden board,
his hands full of the mystery of yeast
and flour—full of Illinois prairie sun,
tan and firm—working gluten lumps
from the raw bread. Crusted toughly—
the loaves he formed—thick-skinned
and earthy. Hard to chew,
harder to swallow.

Last time I bent to kiss his head
the skin was crisp and brown,
a taste of salt rising on my lips,
taking me home, only to leave me
an orphan in the empty kitchen,
the oven open-mouthed and cold.

***

"Swedish Rye" was originally published in *A Stirring in the Dark* (Old Seventy Creek Press, 2012). Reprinted with permission.

The Heart's Dark Rooms
Brenda Yates

I don't know your name, so I'll just say: *Dear*
(woman now) with blue eyes and long slender
fingers, whose birth certificate protects you
from strange names and blanks marked *unknown*.

Though the latter *isn't* true. Truth is: family
(his, mine, ours and, yes, yours) of their time.
Not strong enough to face a small town's long
memories, its tiny cruelties and favorite
pastime of cutting neighbors down to size.

                                     Startled by your beauty,
a mother, young, frightened, but not stupid,
could drop out, get the kind of job one who's
never worked before could get, and raise
a child alone—or give you up.

State wisdom required a wait; the unwed
home at least two postnatal visits. Cheerful
foster parents witnessed your mother's
hands at their door *(so long so slender, just
like hers!)* then passed you on, into adoptive
arms. Before disappeared. True name,
to whom born, sealed by power of the state.

                                    It may be you'd resent
intrusion of the stranger who abandoned you.
But please, understand, you were loved enough
to want *(pray they chose well)* a chance for you.
And I named you. Though it wasn't mandated,
I named you.

Small mirror smiling with my eyes, for years
I've gotten close enough to see the hands
of blue-eyed girls about your age. But it's only

in dreams I find you and secrets come bursting
out: *Jennifer!* Your name is *Jennifer Marie.*

Waiting on My Daughter's Night Class
Carol Barrett

The silversmiths assemble, basement
workshop where the rumble of polishers

does not disturb paramedics in uniform
T-shirts, or mechanics in greasy garb.

I settle in, worn naugahyde couch
in the hall, the comfort of humming

vending machines, finger my options.
Unshaven students come, sip coke,

and go. Some even risk *hello*, or lament
the lack of work, hands in their pockets,

or tilting a blue cap over raised eyebrows.
Once that young, I was taught to say *yes*

to the first man who asked me out.
He'd summoned the courage. Fairness

insisted you went where he led.
Beyond the open classroom door, I hear

the rhythmic tug of rock music, and know,
despite a migraine, my daughter

will not complain to her young teacher,
blue denim shirt sleeves rolled

to the elbows. He coaxes companion
artists — all women — in the contours

of blue wax. One is etching the lines
of a leaf, a real leaf in her lap.

They carve and file, brush, and smooth.
He will mold imaginative jewels,

then fill singular anticipations
with molten silver, pale as first light.

My daughter has formed her first ring.
I hear him admire its balance, its weight,

sundance plane that will glide
on her finger, lift to bluing skies ahead,

carry the knowledge she can leave
any man she chooses.

Packing a Box to Send Home from My Daughter's House in Portland
Shoshauna Shy

Fold in the red dahlias bought
from New Seasons grocery;
bread made from spelt that we
toasted with garlic; emerald
lawns cushioning the orange
and aqua houses.
Pack the voices of the women
in her evening sister circle
whose eyes glinted with joy,
smiles soft and gentle,
shoulders swathed in velvet,
hems kissing ankles.
I pack the song *Shady Grove*
bellowed by her boyfriend;
the banter of a wanna-be
with spilling ginger curls;
the sound of the freight train
through a bathroom window
as it crossed the Willamette
in a pre-dawn chug.
Let me pack our nights asleep
with Tabby Cat on pillows;
the Belmont bus we missed
more than once to campus;
the sweet potato fries,
the chocolate pie we shared;
cherry blossoms caught
in the melody of her laughter;
the silk of our matching stride,
rain misted in her hair.

***

"Packing a Box to Send Home from My Daughter's House in Portland" was previously published in *Verse-Virtual*. Republished with permission.

Playing in the Sprinkler
Patricia Wellingham-Jones

The boy's footsteps, ragged
as his t-shirt is torn, carry him
through dandelions and bright summer grass
to lean against a maple tree
and watch. In the sprinkler
two small children scream and splash.
Their mother, red hair flying,
shorts damp from the play,
beckons him to come join the fun.
Black eyes pooled with pain
in a mocha brown face, he edges
near the spray. Flinches when water
strikes his body. The mother
catches the shudder,
cups his chin, falls into his eyes.
Show me, she whispers, voice gentle as feathers.
His belly and chest seared black
as hot dogs too long on a grill,
the blistered skin peels away
from pink flesh. The mother
sinks to the ground where water beads
can't reach, cradles the burned child
in loose arms. Tries not to drip
salt tears on his seeping wound,
sends her water sprites to the house
for the cell phone.

***

"Playing in the Sprinkler" was originally published in *Interpoetry* (England, 2004). Republished with permission.

Brown Chair
Louis Hoffman

for my father

Smooth leather
Buttoned down and
Curved in all the wrong places
That old brown chair
Stayed at my bedroom desk
Rarely used for homework
Or drawing

Yet each night
If the fear came upon me
I would timidly come into your room
And beckon you to allay the fears
You sat patiently
Occupying that lonely brown chair
That was not built for comfort
If you got up before
My eyes stayed closed
I called out
And you stayed

Each night

You stayed

Such a seemingly simple
Act of love
Staying
Being present
Yet not till my own young son
Timidly came to my bedside
"Papa"
Did I recognize this sacrifice
This act of love
Frustrated and awakened
I remember being held in your love

And I say
"I'm right here, you are safe now."

And I know
Your love has become
My love

***

"Brown Chair" was originally published in *Capturing Shadows: Poetic Encounters Along the Path of Grief and Loss* by Louis Hoffman & Michael Moats (University Professors Press, 2015). Republished with permission.

The Orphan
Juanita Ratner

She's never far away
The pain of her abandonment
Left her afraid
To be alone
And so
You often sense her hovering
About the edges of things
Peeking out for reassurance
And nothing is quite secure enough

If you haven't spoken in a while
She'll ask for a sign
That you still care

How I would reach out to her

But she isolates herself
Afraid to ever know that hurt again

Under my quiet observation
She knows that she is seen
And though she's still afraid to really trust
Today we sat beside a mountain stream
Clear water, rippling and bubbling its way
Through a mountain pass
And the warm embrace of sunlight
Caused her soul to sigh with peace
And open to the beauty
Sustaining all of life.

***

"The Orphan" was originally published in *Searching for My Real Self* by Juanita Ratner. Republished with permission.

Whiskers
Kimberly Weikert

Ever since his father died
he asks the same question,
my little boy —
"who will teach me to shave?"

My little boy —
on his way to becoming a man
is enslaved by the tragedy
that overshadowed his life.

He does not, really
wonder about shaving,
my little boy —
he wonders, fatherless, who will guide him.

We shall stumble
through the stubble
of a beard together —
my little boy and I.

Haiku for a Wanted Child
Christina Lovin

Conceived in winter:
in the cold room warm bodies
gave mutual heat.

Like a gentle drift,
the pillow where you now rest
lifted my bare hips.

Your father's tantrums
when he learns of your coming
flash like silver sleet.

Our roof leaks badly,
but inside me you are safe
from cruel spring showers.

May, I lay alone
on half the vacant bed.
He is gone. You stayed.

Ripe summer belly
veined as a map of the earth,
globed atlas of hope.

Sweet breaking open—
my body an autumn fig
pressing out its seed.

Winter once again:
two bodies under old quilts,
each warms the other.

***

"Haiku for a Wanted Child" was originally published in *ECHO: Poems* by Christina Lovin (Bottom Dog Press, 2014). Republished with permission.

Arguing the Curriculum: Coleslaw
Carol Barrett

My mother is chopping the cabbage
for slaw, coiled heart
held in the spray of her hand,
the blade mincing slivers, infinitely
smaller than my own crude renderings.
Fit for a toddler's teeth, fragrant strips
brushed to one side of the honey-
colored board. She's convinced:
"They don't know what they're talking about.
Opportunities for learning are not enough."
I study her nimble cabbage,
creamy green, wrinkled like her wrists,
the heart holding, bright as the sugar
she will sprinkle into tartness,
the broad knife *thap thap*
as she worries her words toward the table
where I sit. She begins another head.
Thomp. "We have to be sure they can *learn*.
All the fancy courses in the country …"
(perhaps what I teach?) *thap thap*
"won't help a child if he can't
communicate." With this her brows
curl, as if pleading safety for some
unknown waif handing her a cabbage.
I have seen this same face
hover over missing buttons, hooded
carcoat, her thumbs coaxing the needle
toward certain warmth. Nudging
the slaw into a heap, readying the bowl,
she persists, "Humanities don't matter
if you can't figure the groceries.
Some kids nowadays don't know their letters.
They don't even know their colors."
I consider this: the child I found
crying at the airport, unable to give me
her name. It was snowing.
When she calmed to the rainbow

of promises I spoke, she told me
this was her very best dress. Her mother
would be mad if it got lost.
On the counter, the container of sour cream
sweating into the wood, bottle of vinegar,
its tint like plums outside my mother's
kitchen, sunlight clear to the core.
What is the greater wisdom, the greater
need: the fat letters on their ruled lines
or the grace of the cabbage?
My mother opens a carton of milk,
squirt for the slaw. It will finish this.
Prints of lost children fit into her palm.

***

"Arguing the Curriculum: Coleslaw" was originally published in *Feminist Studies, 17*(2), 267–268, 1991. Republished with permission.

Daughter in Her Eighth Month
Felice Aull

Approaching the predicted
midpoint of her life
she is now profoundly pregnant.
It is her first, and no technology
was needed, only the hormones
released by love and a watchful womb.
Grandmotherhood approaches,
a state I did not crave, just as
I did not crave to be a mother
until she thumped her way
into my world, as now her fetal girl—
that floating fingered shadow
the ultrasound detects,
detecting lack which means
she'll have a daughter too—
is pummeling her.
That's how our babes enlist us.
I feel the tiny fingers pull me
into, through, blood on blood,
we three are sliding, slipping toward
the edge of separation.

***

"Daughter in Her Eighth Month" was originally published in *Mom Egg Review*. Republished with permission. "Daughter in Her Eight Month" also was previously published in *Mandatory Evacuation Zone* by Felice Aull (Kelsay Books, 2017). Republished with permission.

My Father
Tom Greening

I remember that last awkward fumbling hug
at the bus stop
when we said goodbye and he knew,
saw what I did not want to see,
that his end was near.
He was an uptight New Englander
and so much more.
When I turned seven
he got me my first dog, sensing
how much I needed one.
He bought me that old Ford
to drive the summer I worked
at the dreary state hospital
where his mother had died.
Now I have lived ten years longer than he did
and wish I could claim
I've given as much.

The Glass of Water
Jeff Santosuosso

My mother returned from her mastectomy
in the evening, left the lights
off, nothing then protecting me
from the darkness inside the hallway
she walked. There was no sight
of Mom's face, her hair, her dress.
She'd put on a bathrobe for dinner,
descended the stairway.
Her full red lips looked thinner
as she clenched and pursed
them like her robe. My first
impression was that they'd never part
for dinner.

She held the glass
the way she embraced me,
the way she graced me
before they found the mass.
The evening, like the water
glass in her hand, passed silent and still
when we children, her son and daughter,
took our homework and studied until
lights out when she unwrapped
the bandages that had trapped
her bound inside. Removing them,
she let go a sigh, laid them neatly side by side
as if she were proving them
worthy of reuse with nothing to hide.

My dad rolled them up, lay them in a drawer, kissed her forehead and
held her as tightly as she would let him, his arms reaching ever so further
around her back as his fingers interlaced, and hers clung onto him as if
he were a glass full of water.

***

"The Glass of Water" was originally published in *Body of Water* by Jeff Santosuosso (Clare Songbirds Publishing House, 2018). Republished with permission.

At the Doorstep
John C. Mannone

              I left my daughter
And her four-year-old little girl
At the emergency shelter.
The intake person seemed to hide
Inside his glass-doored office,
His hard face hidden by dread-
Locks, which curtained smiles
That we didn't know were there
Until he looked up with a soft
Look of compassion. He showed
Us the room at the top of the stairs.
I didn't smell any de-licing powder,
But the stark, spring bunk-beds
Were covered by a dark dust
Of ghosts. He swept it out,
But the haunting and pale
Hopelessness lingered. I felt it
              When I held my baby,
Her face in my hands as if they could
Exorcise her demons and their prince
Of lies. Her tears not washing them out,
I held her at the doorstep of her room,
And making make-believe my tears
Could, I kissed her on the forehead—
An anointing through the hurt
To the innocence I once knew.

***

"At the Doorstep" was previously published in *Keys of Silence* (Cave Moon Press, 2013). Reprinted with permission.

Every Mother's Son
Marcella Remund

We don't lose daughters.
They're strung to our hips
in an invisible web
of women's history:
tin sinks full of dishes,
photogenic half-smiles.

But sons are cut loose
before they can walk.
They teeter on picket
fences between life-sized
cutouts of fathers,
and quaking, fearless mothers.

We give sons sticks and rocks,
shove them out the door,
hope they find their own two feet.
We watch them stumble,
see them read the warnings
we stuffed in clean pants pockets.

Mothers, lock yourselves in
your rooms, hum,
squeeze your eyes shut,
cover your ears.
The boys are flying now,
screeching and golden,
half mother, half man.

Next Steps?
Rodger E. Broomé

I don't know all the steps;
Mine land on your toes.
It is hard to put you through the pain;
I don't know all the steps.

Your limping is hard to watch;
I see your discouragement and struggle.
I have never meant to step on you;
I don't know all the steps.

I disappointed you and let you down;
You once saw your hero, but now a clown.
Nothing is funny but sorry slapstick;
I don't know all the steps.

The memories will always hurt,
But dancing with me won't always pain you.
Daddies and daughters whirl about,
But I don't yet know all your steps, no doubt.

I will do my best to miss your toes;
And I want to lift you high.
Please turn back to me, may I have this dance.
I don't know all our steps, but I want to learn.

Photograph
Maura Snell

Hey, you, in your tutu,
tulle-decked and plump
with the pots of geraniums
leaf-licked and blooming about you—
Hey, you, there, squat on the cement step,
fingers wrapped in fists, bare toes wiggling,
where did you go, little girl?
You surged, opening
the way a new bud might
when placed in water and sunlight
in a fast-frame unfurling.
Will you remember when we are dust?
I can feel how the concrete must have made
your bare skin itch, the leotard, thin
against your tiny bottom pressed down
into rough cement,
already a eulogy.
You've disappeared into gawk and glasses.
But sometimes, when you're not looking,
I squint at you and can still see in your profile
that baby girl,
gazing up at me as she squats
among the geraniums.

***

"Photograph" was originally published in *Brain, Child Magazine* (September, 2015). Republished with permission.

My Father at Ninety-Two, Splitting the Days

Charlotte Mandel

It's five minutes to twelve and the sun
glares in our faces—quite a phenomenon,
he says, to see the windows full of light
and everyone going about—at midnight!
The clock plays second fiddle to his brain.
An hour's nap and he begins the day again,
washes, changes his shirt, and expects
his breakfast on the table. He respects
my worn explaining as a kind of busy
work, shrugs with courtesy. He is dizzy
with the earth's rotation spinning away
twenty-four to the dozen, each brief new day
a clone to the last. Like a match burning
meridians, he strikes his shadow's turn.

***

"My Father at Ninety-Two Splitting the Days" was originally published in *Keeping Him Alive* (Silver Apples Press, 1990). Republished with permission.

Necessary Condolences
Ronnie Hess

I. Old Age

My sister reads the New York Times obituaries
and once again the news is bad.
Another friend's mother is dead.
Yes, she was 100, but three people this month
from the ancestral walk?
And so I have sent the necessary condolences
via Internet guest books, tried to strike
the right note. I sound like someone's playbook,
its rehearsed chapter and verse.
But what I'm really thinking about is
the goodbye waves we gave so wildly
at the boat basin as we set off
for the mainland, swinging our arms
like windshield wipers
over our heads, until our people
and the island vanished.
Or those high-pitched screams we made
in the back of our throats until sound
couldn't travel or we were hoarse.
We were the ones doing the leaving then,
going back to school or to our grownup jobs
in the city. Not them. They were solid rock,
sand and seawater transmuted into cement.
They never told us someday they would be
the ones disappearing, expecting us to bury them,
or politely know how to grieve.

II. Youth

We were after all only children.
We grew up expecting the eternal comfort of parents' laps,
their hands on our bodies smoothing in
protective creams, or brushing our hair back
gently behind our ears.
I don't remember my mother ever saying

prepare yourself, or think of me.
She just kept repeating keep going, keep going.
I took it less for a wish than a curse.
You know what's next.
What's there to do? We're the first line now,
our muskets raised, the enemy just over
the horizon, making its way toward us,
in assured formation, inevitably better armed.

***

"Necessary Condolences" was originally published in *Ribbon of Sand*. Republished with permission.

By Love
Veronica Lac

Not by blood
By choice
By love
She enveloped her and found space in her heart
for her daughter's lost and lonely friend
Absorbing her hurt and disappointments
Shielding her pain
Allowing her space to breathe
To be free from her cultural constraints

This new world
Brings light
Brings hope
to a girl struggling to believe in her right
to exist in this world as she is
Without needing to diminish her own fire
Without pretense
Allowing her to find strength
To be free to explore her experiences

This mother
Believes
Supports
and gives so much of herself to her daughters
Waits in the wings and watches them
take flight, circling, soaring above her
Wondering what life has in store for her now
Perhaps to start
A new venture, a new dream
To be free to give voice to her own hopeful heart

The sisters
Rejoice
Return
from their own flight path to celebrate this dream
To hold the hands that once held theirs
Watching in awe as their mother flies

Witnessing once more her resilience and strength
Knowing that this
is the source of their power
To be free to claim their own right to exist

Not by blood
By choice
By love
This daughter's gratitude, an overflowing well,
Stands as testament to this love
Cemented through mutual choosing
Honored by the generosity of sisters
A mother's gift
A welcoming place to land
To be free, to be loved, and above all, to live.

Hydro Superintendent
Joanne Corey

Each weekday, Dad went to his office
on the top floor of the hydroelectric station,
wearing a clip-on tie —
a precaution due to machinery —
with a Reddy Kilowatt pin.

When he was on weekend call,
my sisters and I sat on the wheel wells
in the back of the company jeep —
wearing our hard hats —
jouncing along unpaved roads
to inspect dams, pipelines, reservoirs,
unmanned Deerfield hydro stations.

His work became ours,
generating power.

***

"Hydro Superintendent" was originally published in the *Binghamton Poetry Project* and on http://topofjcsmind.wordpress.com (Author's Blog). Republished with permission.

The Emerald
Nathaniel Granger, Jr.

Inspired by my adopted son, Theo

When first I saw you
My heart was won
Green is my favorite color you know

Tuesday afternoon
Some Tuesdays ago
I know it was Tuesday
'Cause it was Popeye's parking lot
And I was there for their Tuesday special

A thigh and a leg for $1.14
Or if you prefer white meat,
One wing and a breast for $1.99.
I love fried chicken you know

This kid, called me
Without him knowing
Tickets he was selling
"You wanna buy some tickets to my fight?
I'm a MMA fighter!"

Yes, and, I am going to be
Your number one cheerleader—
Then manager,
Then friend,
Then this

I already had three gems,
A ruby, diamond, and a pearl
The three would argue
Who was the diamond, the ruby, or the pearl?

When God sends a jewel. Recognize
In my heart
My adopted son,

My treasure chest is complete
Eureka! I have found the emerald.

My Imperfect Perfect Son
Louis Hoffman

For all those who share in the experience of Trayvon Martin

My imperfect perfect son
Why did you go walking down there
That fateful night?
You know better,
You know the rules.
Why did you wear those clothes?
If you dress like that,
You better be prepared to act accordingly
Why did you get angry?
And why didn't you just submit?
My imperfect, perfect son
Why?
Why are we now left grieving
After so many wrongs?

My imperfect, perfect son
Why did you go walking down there
That faithful night?
You know the rules are different for you
Some freedoms, in this great country,
You still don't have

My imperfect, perfect son
Why did you wear those clothes?
Those innocent clothes
They do not mean the same thing on you
As they do on a white man of
a certain appearance
Though they serve the same purpose
In the chilly night air

My imperfect, perfect son
Why were you so scared?
And why were you suspicious of this man
Who approached you with a gun?

And why did you let these fears and suspicion
Show as anger?
You know your fears will be dismissed
While the aggressor's will be perceived as real
You know your suspicions are not seen as valid
As the man who chose in advance to hold the gun
You know your anger is never seen as justified
Because of the color of your skin
You are just a child,
But you will be expected
To be the bigger man

My imperfect, perfect son
Why did you think you could live in this world
With the freedoms so many others enjoy
Without question.
You were not free, my son
As our freedom is only within
In how we will respond to the injustices
That constitute the world in which we live in

My imperfect, perfect son
Why are we left grieving
Another of so many wrongs?
Another tragedy befallen on
Our community?
But know, my son
That this wrong will not be forgotten
This wrong will inspire
In this wrong we will find our inner freedom
And in this wrong we will speak out
We will scream out
And we will not stop
Until this inner freedom
Is matched
In the world we must live

***

An earlier version of this poem was published in the January, 2014, *Society for Humanistic Psychology Newsletter* in an article titled,

"Trayvon Martin and Humanistic Psychology: What Does Humanistic Psychology Have to Say About Trayvon Martin?" by Louis Hoffman. https://www.apadivisions.org/division-32/publications/newsletters/humanistic/2014/01/trayvon-martin

"My Imperfect, Perfect Son" was previously published in *Stay Awhile: Poetic Narratives on Multiculturalism and Diversity* by Louis Hoffman & Nathaniel Granger, Jr. Reprinted with permission.

My Son the Artist
Michael Harty

took his grocery budget
to the farmers' market

brought home a perfect
white eggplant

noticed its resemblance
to a giant opal

or an old-fashioned silver airship
or a dinosaur egg

admired it until
it was too soft to eat

i bless every foolish
hair of his head

Wrenhouse

W. F. Lantry

One notes fresh desecrations of the portico,
                    ~Kees

I've made a life of losing everything.
This morning, with my coffee, I looked out
and saw the wrenhouse shattered. When a storm
blew down a cherry limb, I'd taken up
my saw and made a turning blank. The lathe
revolved it gently as a form emerged

and James, excited, asked if he could stay.
I made him sit up on the workbench. When
he waved his arms, I ordered him to keep
his fists thrust into pockets, as I'd done
in my own father's shop when I was four.
He wanted to help sand. I turned it off

and let him run glass paper over wood.
The lacquer flowed on smoothly, and we hung
the whole thing from a tree limb by the deck.
It looked medieval. It looked like it came
from mythic forests, peopled with strange sights.
The wrens soon claimed it. I checked every day

and felt some sadness when they'd raised their clutch
then flew together north in unison.
The birdhouse hung there isolate, and now
this morning, I found pieces of its roof.
Whatever I construct soon shatters. Why
must everything continually fall?

                    ***

"Wrenhouse" was original published in *2010 Ellen LaForge Poetry Prize Annual*, edited by Mary Baine Campbell. (UMB William Joiner Center, 2010). Reprinted with permission.

"Wrenhouse" was previously published in *The Structure of Desire* by W. F. Lantry (Little Red Tree, 2012). Republished with permission.

How It Feels
Alan King

When your mother-in-law takes your daughter
out of her crib after the crying,

after you said she's not hungry 'cause she threw up,
after you told her your daughter rocks to sleep easy but cries
when you put her back,

when your child's grandmother takes her out
after you told her not to,

you remember the rose bush you and
your wife chopped down—the one that blocked
the living room window, that bullied away sunlight—

and you know this grandmother's stubborn
love for her grandchild gashes your authority
the way the thorny bush prickled your hand, arms and legs
in its bold resistance, its open disregard
for what you wanted.

No one tells you parenting is like gardening,
where you defend your choices from parasites posing
as unwarranted advice, where insecurities bred by
judgment and condescension can brown your confidence.

When you watch your mother-in-law holding
your child after you told her not to,

you know how your wife felt that first night home
from the hospital, when your parents came by and
could only seem to unload their criticisms
on how she handled her child.

And if compassion's a deep sorrow for other's misfortune,
do you forgive the know-it-all grandparents their transgressions,
how they selectively forget their mistakes?

Isn't humility an ingredient of compassion,
the one that asks the grandparents to see themselves
as they once were—
green in their new role?

You remember your parents fumbling in the dark
of what they didn't understand, how their trial and
error traumatized your childhood—

how it pushed your brother into a homeless shelter and
his mental illness, your brother spiraling in his orbit of pain,
light years away from forgiveness.

When your child's grandmother takes her out
of her crib, you take your child back, say:
"I love you... but I got this.

***

"How It Feels" was originally published in *Rattle* (#54, Winter 2017).
Republished with permission.

That Time Comes
Patricia Wellingham-Jones

By the time I got there,
ripping away from home and family,
Mother was a bed-bound invalid,
Dad was worn out, faded and gray.

For three weeks he and I rotated
shifts to keep his long-held promise,
that she would be able to stay at home.

In the middle of the night
I leapt up from a heavy sleep
to the crash of oxygen tank,
Dad's thunderous curse,
Mother's terrified wail.

His fatigued and shaking hands
fumbled the changing of the tanks
which tore the oxygen from her face,
ended an era.

Dad and I huddled at the dining room table
spread with files and charts and pills,
faced the next step in their long marriage,
made the tough decision.

In the morning I watched both their hearts break.

A Heart Attack
Michael Waterson

as you toddle toward the stairs,
blissfully oblivious of gravity,
mortality ...

fortified with latches, locks,
and curiosity-proof outlets
the house is under siege as I try

to barricade danger from
those miniature fingers that I suck
and pretend to eat

bumps and bruises land
battalion strong
along with nightmare news –

girl eviscerated by a drain at a pool
plastic bags asphyxiate,
leukemia leaks from TV and toaster

your first word – hot –
taught by the oven door

and I learn words anew
as we move towards common ground
you springing sunward
me in slow declension:
Care Coincidence

Faith that one day soon
you'll stride those stairs
without a second thought,
shrug off the old man's
dotty tales –

Caught you in mid-air!

A Few Unheard Words
W. F. Lantry

"These expectations sour in the sun..."
           -Kees

... And I remember rising before dawn
taking my coffee outside to the shop
thinking I'd be awake enough to drive
at least. Some mornings I wrote florid notes
hoping your registrar would be amused
and not ask pointed questions on the phone.

The books I bought were strewn across your floor
while wind and rain contested wills outside.
Had I done more, repaired the broken crowns
of rented roofs, or snaked the outer drains
perhaps the flood would not have soaked them all
along with clothes, lost papers, magic cards

you kept for years, half hidden from the storm.
But when you asked, I built a greenboard wall
installed a door, made cabinets and a bed,
closet and ceiling: I hoped you would learn
from made example how to build a life
and all the while we discussed the Tao:

you came to me one afternoon and asked
of meaning, and I had no wisdom, so
turned off the lathe, held up a half done piece
and said "a woman who I barely know
will take some small joy in receiving this."
I wish I had an answer you could hear.

St. Dominic
Marcella Remund

patron of choir boys

My sons, three wild choirboys,
have visions too, have wandered
in the fog, brilliant boys who catch
and sing the sun. Their high notes
burst like sparks against a dark
South Dakota sky. Their low notes
disturb the river's calm surface.
Teach them to settle disputes
as you did, with relics—
thumbs or long leg bones planted
in a tenuous line of truce, flag line
between their constant thieving
companions, Need and Want.
Bully them always toward
goodness & mercy.
Knock them down in the
schoolyard if you have to.

What Goes Around
Ellaraine Lockie

... painstaking parents are going to school all the time, and their teachers are their children. from What a Woman of Forty-Five Ought to Know
~ Anna Drake, 1902

I find myself sitting for long spells
in her rocking chair
Prom picture stares suggesting I get a life
beyond golden girl memories
this mausoleum room arouses
With whiffs of lemon scented soap
fading faster than flashbacks
And tombstone trophies that testify
accomplishments from the last child to leave
Toddler turned teacher who tested me daily
Teenager who mentored modern manners
Like how to say *fuck* without mentioning French
And when to forgo formalities
An adult daughter who turns
childhood traumas into survival tools
and defines her own direction
Power she may say learned from me
But my lessons were literate
Ivory tower expertise second-sourced from
Dr. Spock and Gloria Steinem
Myself swaddled in watchkeeper words
A mummy now ready to unwrap
pages of original text
And apprentice in my daughter's
new-woman world
But first a few more minutes to reminisce
before I relinquish the rocking chair

***

"What Goes Around" was originally published in *San Gabriel Valley Poetry*. Republished with permission.

Faerie Panic
Daniel Ari

My kid emerges from her room in tears.
Figure it's another grumpy rising.
Muster pre-coffee patience for her flares.
Wonder what's the plot. Favorite socks missing?
Honey spread too thin? No, she's in despair—

her tooth—fuck me! Her front tooth was waiting
all night long for a distracted fairy.
No cash, not even a note this morning!
The resident spirits negligently
fell asleep entwined, their duties ignored.

She sobs into the shirt she pulls on. We
improvise desperately, stuffing singles
into a red sachet, calligraphy
sign, hot potato it to the fishbowl.
"Hey! What's that by the tank? Is something there?"

She comes, wipes her eyes, collects her windfall.
"Weird," she sniffs. "They didn't use my pillow."

***

"Faerie Panic" was originally published in *One Way to Ask* by Daniel Ari (Norfolk Press, 2016) and *Gold Dust Magazine* (December 2013). https://issuu.com/golddust/docs/issue24_v09small_cover. Republished with permission.

"Faerie Panic" was previously published in *One Way to Ask* by Daniel Ari (Norfolk Press, 2016). Republished with Permission.

Four Months
Alan King

April 29, 2016

Your wife's baby app says at this stage
your daughter should be rolling over and sleeping
six hours straight at night.

Your baby barely sleeps four hours
and when you put her down for tummy time,
she lifts her neck, holds the pose for 10 seconds,
then starts crying.

But you got her sleeping in her crib a month before.

And isn't it a milestone that you and
your wife are friends again?

Night wakings no longer instigate debates
over how much formula to give her, whether
it's too hot for her jumper, or if your wife
should be nursing her every hour.

You both are skilled now in the ninja stealth
of tiptoeing out your sleeping daughter's room.

Even the noisy floorboards that once betrayed you
are no match for your light footwork.

You both are learning the language
of cry tones – the one for hungry,
the one for messy diaper, the one for tired.

Maybe these small triumphs are a way
of keeping you sane when the election cycle
circus and Prince's death make the world
feel like a runaway train.

And just before it seems it's about to jump its tracks,
you remember laughing with your wife over pizza
in your daughter's room – your baby bathed and
ready for bed at a decent hour.

You count your blessings in her high-pitched
wannabe words when your wife says, "Da Da,"
or in the gummy smile she flashes
every time you bump your nose against hers.

Risk
Maura Snell

She lets them sleep together after prom
on the couch in the family room,
their bodies buffered in cotton
curled around each other,
and thinks as she looks in on them
that they still are so small, marvels
that they both can fit
on the long side of the sectional,
her back to his front,
her chin tucked down
into her chest in sleep
like when she was two
and wonders if this is how it will be,
will she always feel like a bad mother
because she lets them stay there at three a.m.,
doesn't usher her daughter off to her own bed,
upstairs, but instead sleeps so well herself,
for once, believing in all that lay
in the crook of that boy's arms.

The Art of War
Shahé Mankerian

The goal of War is to end up
with all of the cards in the deck.
Don't mind the corner creases,

the bite marks – pray for the higher suits.
She doesn't understand and snatches
the five of spades and shrieks,

My age, my card. Napoleon said, *Ignore*
the tantrum of the young lieutenant.
My shuffle resembles the repeated

slices of the guillotine. A black,
two-headed king falls out of the stack.
She picks it up. I remind her to hold

the cards face down. But my daughter,
like the other disoriented queens, seems
fixated by the crippled king without feet.

Bird-Boy: Eve Remembering Abel
Charlotte Mandel

I could have killed him
that time—
"Ma-a, watch me fly!"
His knuckly toes
gripped the edge of the quarry
Vertical drop
to the gloating green eye of water
I saw his shirt fly off
his navel, the dimple and crack
of flat buttocks

Every mother carries murder in her heart
"Ma-a, look at me-e . . ."
arms outstretched like the flight bones
of a bat's skeleton

I was screaming his name by then
breath spurting from my mouth like blood
I stood too far below to stop him in time
too far above the water to race down
billow the safety net of my skirt
"Ma-a, look at me-e . . ."

His name
wailing thin from my lungs

Into the air he leapt
arc of an eagle
his cry a mosquito whine

"A-a-a-be-l-l . . ."
mocked back from the stones
like bursts of laughter.

Bird-boy
silhouetted on water
divided the gleaming surface and came

gliding the way a web-footed bird
seems to propel with its belly.

I wanted to beat him for my gasping heart.
Perched to dry in the sun, he cocked his head—
"Tell me a story about
when you were a little girl."

There is no such story.
No childhood begins me.
I thought story was mine to create
by what I lived.

Abel my son
knew himself invulnerable
to powers of rock, water, a mother's
righteous blows, her rebel's
rage against the story-weaver
who had named him
the one who would be killed by his brother.

***

"Bird-Boy: Eve Remembering Abel" was originally published in *Sight Lines* (Midmarch Arts Press, 1998). Reprinted with permission.

Insomnia Immediately Post-Partum
Marion Deutsche Cohen

How can I possibly
when each time I do
I dream the nurse brings in the baby?
Or my other children?
Or my husband?
How can I possibly
when each time I do
life-sized cardboard pictures of yellow Wildthings torment me?
and every object I grasp
shrinks?
and a jack-in-the-box, again and again
each time doubling in size?
How can I possibly
when each time I do
somebody yells, Wake up?

***

"Insomnia Immediately Post-Partum" was previously published in *The Fuss and the Fury* by Marion Deutsche Cohon (Alien Buddha Press, 2019). Republished with permission.

Inside, Looking Out
Felice Aull

Lightling, chirped my baby girl
when I named the silver flash
slicing the sky.
I held her in the crook of my arm
as we looked out
through the living room window.
Drawn there by gathering darkness
and grumbling thunder, I showed her
rain streams bouncing on asphalt,
brilliant light strikes, waited
for explosions to follow.
Torrents battered the windows
but we were safely cocooned, the spectacle
enlivening our day. *Lightling*,
I say now, years later,
seeing the flash.

***

"Inside, Looking Out" was originally published in *Mandatory Evacuation Zone* by Felice Aull (Kelsay Books, 2017). Republished with permission.

Counterpoint
Carol Barrett

My six-year-old has saved a gray mouse
from being eaten alive, out of the cat's
mouth like a fish hook, holding
his ears back. He had pawed it
all across the rug, claw-pricks
she wet with a bowl of water
from her play kitchen. *I holded him
on my chest and he didn't run away!*

    *

My daughter cannot know how I too
have kept awake for a thumping
far faster than my own beat minding
the hours, how I have charted
the dipping frequency of thumb-print
kicks, irregularities in pitch
and tone, hearts like a tandem
bicycle, lub-dup lub-dup underlying
pum-bum pum-bum pum-bum pum-bum.
She cannot know how I have memorized
this music precisely, point
by counterpoint, felt the thin
mask of oxygen as rhythm rearranged
itself, the quick beat slowing almost
to a match, disappearing in the fog,
then resuming like a train around a bend,
the nurses' faces pretending to hide
what they know, the way they signal
each other with minimum alarm,
the staccato pianissimo of code words,
a gurney arriving in my room, one
side split down in a split-second.

    *

I imagine this the same ecstasy of nuns
in a summer rain, habits fluttering like peach
blossoms in the wind, or a hailstorm

in the middle of Kansas that keeps
coming, and coming, yes the ecstasy
of a congregation of crickets beneath
a tree-house before the call to supper,
of ferris wheels rocking the sky blue
and blue, of ferns unfurling their long
slow curls to the sun, of the first
grass knot tied for the first doll.

  *

My daughter knows only that she hid
the mouse in the hall closet,
imagines him there still, rumpling
winter scarves and mittens, building
a mouse house with play kitchen,
a jungle gym made of hangers and old ties.
She imagines he is forever safe
in the world, this very moment
nestled in, watching the latest
little mouse video, munching popcorn.

  *

As I imagine pum-bum pum-bum
my little girl, my thimble-
hearted baby, forever breathing.

***

"Counterpoint" was originally published in *Poetry Northwest*, XLI(3), 41–42, 2000. Republished with permission.

"Counterpoint" was previously published in *Mourning Sickness: Stories and Poems about Miscarriage, Stillbirth, and Infant Loss* edited by Missy Martin (Omniarts Press, 2008). Republished with permission.

Brushing My Mother's Teeth
Christina Lovin

Not what you might think. Not those
I remember only from photos
of a gap-toothed young woman.

Solid, these are held in my hand: soiled—
yellow and caked with starch from nursing
home food. The brush sends out specks that stick

to the faucet, spot the break-proof mirror
in the tiny shared toilet. Another woman
mumbles incoherently on the other side

of the cheap laminate door, while water runs
clear now around the precise shape
of my mother's shrunken gums, sloughing

the smooth channel, rinsing clean each tooth,
perfect save for the chip hewn from the left front
incisor; and I remember her foot—

wet, dripping warm, scented
water back into an enamel basin,
then gently rubbed, lovingly patted

dry to be followed by the other.
The foot washer rising, untying
the long linen towel kept just for this

sacred observance. I see my mother accept the cloth,
winding it around her waist, then kneel
before the next woman in the circle.

Takes her foot, lifts it by a callused heel
into the washbowl between them.
I watch bored, too young to participate,

not understanding then those offices of humility
one will stoop to out of duty or tradition,
and on occasion, some reverent love.

***

"Brushing My Mother's Teeth" was originally published in *ECHO: Poems* (Bottom Dog Press, 2014).

The Mother of the Bride Smiles
Phyllis Wax

Beautiful, isn't she, coming down the aisle?
Forget those weeks of confrontation,
of being berated for speaking up and
then again for keeping quiet. Just smile,

at all times, smile. Look past
the points of tension and reinvent yourself
as someone without opinions, someone quiet
and agreeable. Get beyond the vast

amount of time and money
spent on manicures and pedicures,
on clothes, food, music, on invitations—
all the superficialities of matrimony.

My bloodied tongue is salty and sore,
yet I smile and smile, and smile some more.

Daddy–Daughter Dance
Lisa Xochitl Vallejos

I watched her heart
Break all over
Marble floors
tears spilled down
her still chubby cheeks
when she wondered
why her daddy doesn't love
her anymore
and she had no date to
the daddy–daughter
dance

The Night He Broke His Collarbone
Leah Browning

The diaper commercials never show
all the waiting:

the outer room at the dentist or
the living room when he's out late or

at his bedside, in the emergency room,
waiting to take the X-rays or hear the results.

Or now, standing outside in the driveway
in the dark, waiting for the ambulance.

My son is sitting in the front
passenger seat of my car,

trying not to move too much
or cry or throw up, and

I stand in the wedge of light
from the car's open door.

Earlier tonight, when the sun was still low,
he hit a bump on the BMX track

and slammed into the ground
shoulder-first. He is not quite thirteen.

His friend had to borrow a cell phone
to call his father and ask him to drive over

and pick them up in his SUV.
At the time, it didn't seem so serious.

The neighbors have come outside,
one already in her nightdress and robe,

wringing her hands. There is nothing left
to say. Mostly, it is quiet. Other cars drive past,

and at the end of the street, a city bus stops
to collect its passengers before grinding away again.

One night, on a school trip, there was an accident—
but it was twenty years ago and all I remember now

is filing off a bus in the dark, and seeing
a teenage boy laid out on his back

in a parking lot, in some unfamiliar state—
in another lifetime, it seems now.

But it is all called back by the faint sound of the siren
rising from the bottom of the hill,

eliciting a familiar sense of relief. The ambulance
pulls to a stop in front of us, and the back doors are opened

to reveal its inner workings: the raised white cot,
the long gray bench, a series of cupboards, and then

the confident, efficient machine of the paramedics
emerging with their clipboards and backboard

and gloves and stethoscope,
and the pair of silver scissors they'll use

to cut his shirt off his body, deftly,
like magicians performing a deceptively complex trick,

and in that moment I almost expect to see rising smoke
and a flurry of milk-white doves

as they set aside the glittering mirror of the scissors
and whisk back the colored cloth.

***

"The Night He Broke His Collarbone" was first published in *Eunoia Review* (November 14, 2013), https://eunoiareview.wordpress.com/2013/11/14/the-night-he-broke-his-collarbone/. Republished with permission.

"The Night He Broke His Collarbone" was previously published in *In the Chair Museum* by Leah Browning (Dancing Girl Press, 2013). Republished with permission.

"The Night He Broke His Collarbone" was previously published in *The Wardrobe* (blog). Featured on April 28, 2014.

Binky Bond
Marilyn Zelke Windau

You came home,
those days before the wedding,
before your sisters arrived.
We placed names and curly twig bits
on cards, favor boxes,
stamped blue chrysanthemums,
pressed ribbons into place.

After you were gone,
I found them together in your room.
Under a big blue comforter,
in 75 degree summer cool
after 93 degree humidity,
there they were:
your pink baby binky with tattered lace
and wide satin binding
folded snuggly atop two threadbare thin
blue striped blankies,
mine from childhood.

Did you know?
Did they seem to be right united?
Was there more comfort in their together touch?
Did you realize that your mother's love
will always be there to warm you—
that softness ages us onward to dreams?

Light Rain
Annie Lighthart

Stern voices in the world say they know what matters most
but I find I don't know anymore.

Once I'd have said it was love — it would have been so good,
so fine to say and I would have believed it was true.

But this morning the baby is screaming
and my son bitterly complaining
while their father, besieged, tucks and buttons their clothes.

I take a spider outside in a glass
and kneel in almost invisible rain until it climbs
into the grass and is gone.

Now I see it has been tenderness all along. Now I am ready to fail,
to go back inside and begin it again.

***

"Light Rain" was originally published in *Iron String* (Airlie Press, 2013). Reprinted with permission.

Skating with Our Daughter on Veteran's Day
Carol Barrett

He was born from soil beneath this ice,
clay red with tears, the names of tribes
calling now as I watch his broken back:
Winnebago, Hopi, Sioux. Witness:
we broke his back in Nam,
where the boys skated on mud.
He could not keep them
from falling. He pinned tags
on their stiff toes,
and sent them home.

At least the bones went back.
We broke his back in Nam,
and before that – we broke it.
I watch his stooped ghost
travel this ice, racing
his brothers across their backyard
river, his grandfather's black hair
trailing the Mississippi.

I am here to witness. At least the bones
went back. Not always so:
Cherokee, Chickasaw, Choctaw.
Bones shipped in small
white parcels to stone museums.
Artifacts, we call them:
leather, flint, bone. The severed hands
of his fathers now in Paris,
feet in Munich, ribs scattered
to Rio de Janeiro and Rome.

They are calling in the bones:
Chinook, Cheyenne, Santee,
assembling the teeth,
the wrists of his people,
returning the dead beneath the ice,

raising them high above the snow
in the rattled air of ravens
so souls can rest, his grandfather,
his mother, all the mothers.

Smoke rises:
Makah, Iroquois, Shawnee.
New fires by the ice. Old bones.
In the capital city
the Nations weep, calling
for clavicle, hip bone, skull.
Bones in the Smithsonian
still haunt their graves.
Federal skeletons, exempt
from law: *Pawnee, Delaware, Osage.*
There is no release.

My daughter's small bones on skates
make tiny drums on the ice:
Yakima, Penobscot, Creek.
Her father glides toward me,
back rising, long hair
clinging to his face, lifts her
into the net of my bones.

***

"Skating with our Daughter on Veteran's Day" was originally published in *Calling in the Bones* by Carol Barrett (Ashland Poetry Press, 2005). Republished with permission.

"Skating with our Daughter on Veteran's Day" was previously published in *Whirlwind Magazine*, #4, May 15, 2015. Republished with permission.

Crossing from One Continent to the Next
Leah Browning

Had I known how much time would pass before we'd see each other again, I would have said a different goodbye.
         ~ Karen Thompson Walker, *The Age of Miracles*

There is no way to know how many hours you have
spent awake, pacing up and down the hallway
outside my bedroom door. All night, perhaps,
the thoughts scattered and gathered again,
circling in the darkness like small, restless birds.

I find you at dawn. I have been afraid for so long
that it is almost a relief to come to the end, to know
that we have finally reached the distinct separation
between water and land. You are a stranger now,
and we no longer speak a common language,

but this seems somehow unsurprising, inevitable.
Without knowing it, all these months, we've been
preparing to cross the ocean at night, and the fear
of leaving is only less than the fear of staying still.
By the time the ambulance arrives at the office,

it is close to dinnertime, and you've worn yourself
hoarse. All day, I have seen occasional flickers of you,
of the person I remember, as one might catch
a glimpse of a stone or shell beneath a shallow wave
before the ocean water carries it out of sight again.

There are two paramedics, and they help you onto a gurney
and tie you down with straps. You are shaking,
despite your jacket, and they cover you with a heavy
blue blanket. We will not be allowed to go inside
the hospital tonight, so we have to let them lift you

into the back of the ambulance and close the doors.

The grass grows high under my feet, seasons change,
this world becomes another world. I grow old and die
a thousand deaths and still I go on standing there,
watching that ambulance take you away from me.

***

"Crossing from One Continent to the Next" was first published in *Amygdala*, Volume 1 (May 14, 2015), https://amygdalalitmag.wordpress.com. Republished with permission.

"Crossing from One Continent to the Next" was previously published in *Out of Body* by Leah Browning (Dancing Girl Press, 2018). Republished with permission.

Fruit of Stories
Carol Dorf

Demeter and her daughter Persephone:
every woman tells this story with her mother.
Temptation of the thin-skinned juice-filled seeds,
and following that God back to Hades,
wrapping arms around his leathery waist,
as the motorcycle shoots through time and space.

We return to mother with our children,
but she puts the plates of soup in front of them,
while we peel fruit, and rinse scummy glasses.
We say, "I didn't know it would be like this,"
and she smiles, folds a towel, and starts humming
a lullaby we could remember if only she'd been patient.

Our daughters won't stop growing; our laps grow
crowded with these half-woman girls. They say, "No!"
when they see breasts softening their bony ribs.
We reply, "It can't be helped." We'd like to stop
feeding them hard-boiled eggs, but they've developed
a taste for that mix of rubber and mush.

We can't close the door or hold back the day
they cut a pomegranate off the tree,
and run through the fields in search of a God.

The Child
Juanita Ratner

She never quite relaxes
Waiting for you to criticize
Needing your approval
Afraid to try
Afraid to fail
The sun is veiled by the clouds in her eyes.

She needs a hug
But is afraid to ask.

And if by chance
Someone looks a little
Deeper
And sees
The love
The wisdom
The beauty and spirit
Which shine
Irrepressibly
When she forgets herself
She runs away.

I want to tell her
It's all right now
No one can REALLY hurt you
Anyway
But she has known the truth of suffering
So it's better to hold her while she feels
Her pain
Perhaps it was the aloneness that was devastating
All the time.

Sometimes I bring her into the garden with me
And protect her
While she plays among the flowers
And feels the warmth of the sun on her back
And the breeze kissing her bare arms.

I wish I could share with her
The Peace
Where safety dwells
Where it's all right to ask
And everyone is just becoming
The light and love flow from heart to heart
And all souls recognize their
Home.

***

"The Child" was originally published in *Searching for My Real Self* by Juanita Ratner. Republished with permission.

The Talk
Louis Hoffman

For my sons

We have to talk,
my son
No, it's not the sex talk,
that will come
and don't worry,
no one has died
Well, that's not what this is about
But it is a talk that I
don't know how to have
and a talk where I
don't know what to say
We have to talk, my son
about the color of your skin

You see, my son, your whole life
we've told you that your skin
is beautiful
that you can be proud of who you are:
white and black
We've encouraged you to treasure
the cultures that shaped you
and that you
have nothing to be ashamed of

But you see, my son, that's only
part of the story
and now you need to know
the rest of the story

My son, the world has not been taught
the wisdom your mummy and I
tried to instill;
it is not yet ready to hear
And the world…
Well, the world

will treat you differently
they will follow you in stores
they will perceive you as suspicious;
any anger, no matter how just,
will be seen as threatening
Some will not want you to date their daughters
no matter how proper
and respectful you are
and people will say things
and these things will hurt,
but they will not apologize
and may even accuse you
of being too sensitive
or dismiss you altogether
At times, my son, you may question who you are
because of this unjust world around you

I fear, too, my son
that I have not been a good role model
My skin is not like yours
and I have often taken advantage
I have not kept my hands on the steering wheel
when pulled over for speeding
I have not shown you what to do
when followed in a store -
it has not happened to me
I have not hesitated to be bold in righteous anger
and I have not told you
that if you do the same,
it will be received differently

My son,
you are living in a world
I do not know
I have tried to learn
but my lessons are not as deep
as the ones you will come to know

Please know, my son, that I have tried
I have tried to change the world
I have tried to make it

so that we would not have to have
this talk
I have tried in my anger
and I have tried in my tears
I have tried with some success
and I have tried with some cost
I have fought and fought
and each time I think of you
I have fought more
But I have failed,
and I failed again
I am sorry

My son, this is a beautiful world
and you, too, are part of that beauty
but it is not the world that I want for you
I don't have the answers
but I will walk with you
for as long as God grants me the grace
to be with you.
I will scream out with your anger
and I will cry with your tears
And though my love was not strong enough
to change the world for you, my son,
know that I will never waver
as you walk this world of tears.

***

"The Talk" was previously published in *Stay Awhile: Poetic Narratives on Multiculturalism and Diversity* by Louis Hoffman and Nathaniel Granger, Jr. (University Professors Press, 2015). Republished with permission.

Walk
Marilyn Zelke Windau

My dad used to say
we all needed to walk a mile
in another man's moccasins.
I had moccasins.
They were hand-me-downs.
They were Minnetonkas.
They were smooth earth ochre,
comfortable,
with soft fleecy linings.
I had never walked a mile before.
I walked until I cried,
and then sat down on the trail.
I could have been picked off
by the proverbial bobcat,
who strikes the weakest link.
There were no lurking predators
that day in the north woods.
Dad picked me up and carried me
the last feet of the journey.
It's hard to walk a mile
in another man's moccasins.
My dad walked them first for me.

***

"Walk" was previously published in *Hiccups Haunt Wilson Avenue* by Marilyn Zelke Windau (Kelsay Books, 2018). Republished with permission.

The Message
Annie Lighthart

The urge to fall down, to stumble into sleep, is very strong
but not as fierce as a crying baby in your arms,
an angry force gathering steam, a miniature bellow
stoking his own sound, bald head sticking out from the blanket
like a tiny old man's, furious that his slippers are missing
and his dinner is cold. He too would sleep
if not for the press of the complaint, the rage and the roaring.
He is telling us something, telling us hard, his eyes squeezed shut
with the force of the tale. It could be war or storm
or prophetic expostulation: you are lost to it,
bewildered, almost weeping yourself as you lie on the bed
with him right beside you, a small radio gone mad,
an urgent broadcast, all night long one untranslatable station.

Morning, Third Sunday in June
Phyllis Wax

The call comes
as though planned
just as I cut into a yolk
"Hi, Mom"

and on the horizon
I see a scrap of sail

I know better
than to say "My eggs
are getting cold, can I call you back?"
because her voice has the scent
of a cloud, a wisp of the wind
which is pushing the sail closer

Casually we share our weekend
but soon there is no more to say—after all
we spoke just yesterday

On the water
the sail luffs,
a voice warns
"Coming about"

"Happy Father's Day,"
she says, "Thanks for being both"

The yolk is a loud lump
upon my plate

***

"Morning, Third Sunday in June" was originally published in *Free Verse* (May/June 2003) and was also published in the Silver Boomer Books anthology, *On Our Own: Widowhood for Smarties*. Republished with permission.

Photograph, 1975
Christina Lovin

My mother in a red coat, reclining
in the prow of a gray row boat. Gray all around.
Gray the sky. Gray the water. Gray her eyes,
although my father always called them blue.
This, in their fiftieth year together—
the children grown and gone—my father unseen
behind the camera. My mother's look coquettish
and young as any lover in this autumn shot.

Thirty years later, ten years past his death—
her health gone, four of seven children gone, gone
that bloom about her which even I, the youngest,
remember—she wastes in bed to skin and broken bone.
Your father was a keeper, she states one day
for no apparent reason. Him being only Father to me
I fail to understand. Until, when going through her things,
I pull this photo, whole, from a box of ruined prints.

***

"Photograph, 1975" was originally published in *A Stirring in the Dark* by Christina Lovin (Old Seventy Creek Press, 2012). Republished with permission.

My Mother's Power
Felice Aull

is so great
years after she is dead
that seconds pass
before I startle to catch myself
speaking to her inside my head,
left to cast about—no one else
quite right for my news.

***

"My Mother's Power" was previously published in *Mom Egg Review*. Reprinted with permission. "My Mother's Power" was also previously published in *Mandatory Evacuation Zone* by Felice Aull (Kelsay Books, 2017). Republished with permission.

The Smell of Pine
John C. Mannone

                I

My father was taller than a pine tree
when I climbed into his arms.

I held his limbs, looking down
pining the uprooted ground.

I pressed against his face, rough as bark,
whiskers stiff as bristle cones.

Yet he was a whispered kiss, a gentle wind,
the caress of leaves, the smell of evergreen.

                II

Now it's my turn to bear the pine-tarred tree.
I help him climb on me, his body frail.

I hold Dad, pressed hard against
the wooden box, then return him

as he has done for me so many times—
to the safety of the ground, to soft needles.

***

"The Smell of Pine" was previously published in the *Peacock Journal* (http://peacockjournal.com/john-c-mannone-five-poems/). Republished with permission.

Private Enterprise
Marion Deutsche Cohen

I reach out my hand.
Elle at 7 hugs the notebook.
"It's PRIvate," she says.
"You can't read it because it's PRIvate."
"Aw come on, I shrug. I'm a writer, too. You know
 I'll understand."
"That's not the point, Mom. It's a diary; it's supposed to be PRIvate."
"You mean, anything that goes into it, I can't know about. But
 suppose it's something I could have helped with."
"Oh, you can KNOW about it. I'll tell you all about it. You just can't
 READ it, that's all. It's just
 that it's PRIvate. You can't read it because it's PRIvate."

Sleeping Child
Charlotte Mandel

My gaze cannot mark you
while you sleep.

Your face in still relief
lashes precise as thorns
warn me away
from fastened lids.

Your daylight eyes reflect
the cutting points of mine.
I see you turn, trying to save
your edging core
and yet

moment by moment
I chisel at your image.

I fear to pierce, I fear to flaw
and I fear
to break the watch.

Lips parted
you breathe

asleep

invulnerable.

Watch
Maura Snell

Another child has gone missing.
This time, in Texas.
They say she was last seen
riding her bike in the park.
Last week it was a girl from Colorado;
eleven years old, raped,
dismembered in a coalfield.

So when I tell you I watch you
from the window as you wait
at the corner for your ride to school
it's because it's hunting season
and you are a gazelle
at the edge of the shining water
and in the tall grass on the fringe
of the woods there are tigers
sniffing for your scent in the air.

Mom Raps Me on the Knuckles
Lois Marie Harrod

I am sitting at the kitchen table
looking at my hands,
your knuckles, Mom,
what's left of you.
Today it rained.
Why does the body
shrink in the coffin?
Silly question
for someone like you
who preserved heaven
as she dried peaches.
We'll all have something sweet
in the by and by.
I have your letters,
the same journal week to week,
unreflective as an almanac.
What did you do
when your hand
could no longer rap?
Today I made strawberry preserves.
Today I processed the tomatoes.
I am sadder for my daughter
than you ever needed to be for me.
Today I scrubbed the tiles.
Today I scrubbed the kitchen sink.
What is there but knuckles,
the knuckling down
to the job at hand?

Comforting Jack When He Wakes Coughing and Crying with a Cold
Charles Rossiter

cheek to beard we sway
our breathing slow

slower...
I tell him about the day

the moon, anything
it's not the words

it's our shadow on the wall
night whispers around us,

he is old enough to hold me
as I hold him, close

we grow heavy together,
almost asleep, I put him down

pull the cover up around him.

***

"Comforting Jack When He Wakes Coughing and Crying with a Cold was previously published in *No, I Didn't Steal This Baby, I'm the Daddy* (A. P. D., 1995). Republished with permission.

Sea Creatures
Patricia Wellingham-Jones

for Marty

Sturdy as a bollard, she crouches
beside a tide pool. Lug soles grip rock
slippery with braided ribbons
and air-puffed bulbs of just-flung seaweed.

With the gentle stroke of a mother's finger
on baby skin, she stirs the cupful of life
caught in the salt-crusted rock bowl.
Raises eyes brimming Pacific green.

On her back, snug in the rising wind,
her first-born, late-born daughter sleeps.
Only days from her swim in mother
fluid, the infant cells fill with fresh sea air.

For this pair the swirl of the tide
is hardly distinguished from their heartbeats,
skin drenched with ocean spray, rinsed in falling rain,
as natural to them as tea by a landlubber's fire.

***

"Sea Creatures" was originally published in *FZQ* (2001). Republished with permission.

After She Tells You
Maura Snell

she dreams of killing herself
even the light from the lamp feels different.
The glow from the bulb is frigid.
You don't know how to reach her. She is
a whole other species, this woman-child, who used to sit
pig-tailed and covered in pancake syrup in your kitchen.
The doctor's office is both tomb and haven,
her eyes mask and mirror.
                          They remind you
of blue blossoms behind your mother's house,
how you used to run through tall grass,
let weeds sting your arms as you filled them
with wildflowers. They never lasted:
they would wilt before you made it home.
You remember how you wore dresses every day,
hand-stitched pinafores, hair secured in barrettes,
ruffled socks inside brown lace-up shoes.
They looked solid on your feet, as if
they could take you anywhere. And here you are.
                          And she lay beside you,
your daughter, as small as she was born.
You pretend you know exactly what will happen next
with the calm assuredness of your yesterday self—
you have no idea.

The College of Mothers
Shoshauna Shy

Is this not proof, this report
from the emergency clinic
that conducted dilation
and curettage?
Never mind the babies
hours old in my arms
that I rose to present
to the cluster of in-laws

      when that day before Christmas
      blood coursed down my legs
      and the nurse gently proffered
      the pan that contained him –
      he scallop-sized with ankles crossed

granting me admission
to that college of mothers,
not the one where women bear
and raise children
but where they carry always
the ones that they lost.

                ***

"The College of Mothers" was originally published by *Santa Clara Review* (Volume 99, No. 1, 2012). Republished with permission.

"The College of Mothers" was previously published in *ExpressMilwaukee.com* (November 15, 2012). Republished with permission.

"The College of Mothers" was previously published in *The Splash of Easy Laughter* by Shoshauna Shy (Kelsay Books, 2017). Republished with permission.

The Interview
Michele Riedel

Shoes, belt coiled, shirts
and ties laid smooth like runways
semester's over—he's home.

Finding old polish
he rubbed into the pores
of scuffed shoes and skin
until fingers ache
into a hard shine.

Borrowed folder
leather pockets hold dust
seeping into tightly gripped edges
of rehearsed answers
and sweaty replies.

Next to overloaded laundry basket,
he stands
mirror shined shoes
jacketed with runway tie
ready.

He spins quarters in his pockets
with a smile like 1000
rhododendrons outside.
Toe tips out
he rocks back on his heels
—Johnny Jump ups
springing toward the May sky.

I watch him leave
like that first day driving
alone.
Puddled in the window,
while hangers punctuate chairs
over an array of jackets.

Father Hunger
Michael J. Gargano

Father Hunger is the name.

I come from a long line of men whose fathers were lost and could not speak.

I was born in a time when men were not invested in raising their children.

I am cold

distant

unavailable.

My child, that hunger you feel deep within you comes from me. You want to fill the hunger but it is impossible.

Drugs, alcohol, sex, money, television, cars, violence, crime, gambling, sports, and education are all ways to escape the pain of hunger.

But I am relentless.

You cannot fill this hole by yourself. Many before you have tried without success.

Your desire to understand me leads you to more questions.

But they cannot be solved.

You enter therapy to find out why you are so angry and restless and discover that it is me again —

Father Hunger.

I told you cannot push me away.

Your quest to understand me has given you opportunity to look inward and sense the hurt and pain you've been suppressing.

Where has my father been? you ask.

Silence fills the room.

You pray that the hunger will no longer be.

Father Hunger never goes away.

You wonder what you could have done different or what to have changed.

The answer is nothing.

You realize you did nothing wrong.

Father Hunger teaches you to do things on your own.

If I have taught you anything it is to not be like me when you have children.

Don't model after me.

Remember the lessons you have learned from Father Hunger.

Distance makes the heart grow hungry and searches for answers.

Is that what you want your children to grow up with?

Father Hunger comes from the old ways of doing things.

But now you have a choice to follow in my footsteps

or to change.

What kind of parent do you want to be?

Return
W. F. Lantry

Two deer graze underneath those windmill trees
as James and I go by. We stop. One's head
rises from browsing, looks. The other turns
towards us, then away. Her tail flips
a pulse of white, and quickly she recedes
into the undergrowth, and then she's gone.

Someone comes up behind us. We move on.
I glance back, and the first is staring still
along our path. James notices, and seems
as if he'd linger, fascinated by
her motionless but animated form,
but we turn for our destination now.

I drop him at the door. He makes me vow
we'll soon return to that catalpaed hill
as if we could remake the time, transform
some future moment back, renew the seeds
of what he felt, and cultivate the slips,
the cuttings of emotion, reinvent

the feelings of that instant we had spent
to make them bloom again. And I would try
to populate the landscapes of his dreams
with leaves that deer could browse when she returns,
but know exactly why she, silent, fled
and have no words to remake what he sees.

***

"Return" was originally published in *The Structure of Desire* by W. F. Lantry (Little Red Tree, 2012). Republished with permission.

Rehearsals
Brenda Yates

I'd like to reassure him, tell him happy endings in some
glorious place where everyone is whole again, or bring

back magic with a kiss that banishes hurt. But he's six,
beyond all that, and turns away, inconsolable because

he's figured out that everyone has to die: *All my friends!
You and Dad, too...even sooner!* Not so very long ago,

he would check my reaction to anything strange or loud.
Holding him in my arms, I'd explain; he'd put his hand

on my cheek, watching my face like no one ever has.
And when at five his whys and whats and hows emptied

us of our certainties, our heads bent together over books
of dinosaurs, whales, volcanoes or stars to fill the void.

Deciding that we both must have been absent on the day
kindergartners learn about taste buds, he drew a sectioned

tongue then used ours to demonstrate with lemon, sugar, coffee and
salt. At the zoo, while land tortoises mated,

honking, clacking their shells, he shook his head amused
as child after child got jerked away by grownups who raised

their voices—and kept talking to cover the urgent noises. Silly, he said.
And how impatient when we were slow   giving

human details: *Just tell me **how** the seed gets fertilized!*
Cloaked in the simple faith of his childhood, we were   unaware.

Complexities had been squirreled away in a secret place
beyond our knowing. Unfrocked, my head fills with noise.

Look both ways. Don't talk to strangers. Never swim alone and not
too soon after a meal. Always cut away from your

hand. All these things thrown after him, like confetti, because I knew:
one day he would sail away. But not that

he was already leaving.

Impelled Toward Light
Carol Barrett

I carried only the weight of my mother's
instruction: get a good tree.
My father's hatchet strapped to his belt,
Lady's ears perked for the gambit,
we crossed the highway and skittered
rocks on the old logger's run
to Beaver Dam. Storm timbers
catapulted over the road, still greening:
some we ducked and some we straddled,
the pitch gumming our senses, the path now
a grassy funnel. I tagged spruce,
then pine, height and girth weighed out
in the echoing gorge: poor match
for the fullness of my father's vision.

The year before, my mother disenchanted
with his lean choice, he drilled holes
in the trunk, stuffed boughs to fill
the bare space. Grafted branches don't bend
with the grace of native;
the want in his gift stuck out
in all directions. This year:
a noble fir, grown deep under the forest
roof, its young trunk made to seek the light
slowly, not in quick summer spurts
sprawling skyward. He was after
a burly prize, thick with competition.

So we took to the brush,
salmon berry and bramble, boulders
and lightning-split stumps sprouting ferns,
scalloped fungus. I followed my father's
lead as it trained on it, tree to tree
on the steep bank, heady with exuberance,
the prick of Oregon grape.

Not knowing where we were, I figured
the oozing gullies to lead dam-ward
somewhere below. My father's compass
fixed on another pole: my mother's pleasure.
Knees to the slope, humus sliding
over red clay, I reveled in keeping up,
knew the light was leaving, certain
of the gauge: his hand on the horizon.
Soaked in tiredness, I pulled up
on the nearest flounce, wondered
how we'd haul it, back over the wild,
the wake of tripped blackberry.
Still in pursuit, his hair whiskered
with needles, suddenly my father understood
Lady was not with us. He assumed
the child would know the dog's
boundings, furry troop on our flank.
I assumed he knew what mattered:
where the beaver live, where the best
trees grow, where we were, all of us.
In that moment, more than Lady was lost.

There is a shade of darkness they call
pitch black, and in that shade
we came finally to the house,
hatchet still unsheathed.
He carried her wet wool form
all the way back, angling up the cliff,
deciding dark would beat us
on the old road. I grew up hearing
when lost on a mountain, follow
a stream out. Here, that saving
principle in reverse, working
but without precision: to climb
at night is to crawl.

First light, my mother's face:
the same frozen agony, that day
my sister disappeared on Klipsan Beach
headed for the lighthouse.

My father ran fresh water for Lady, left
me to explain, all that time, no tree.

Years later I took my first lover
down the road to Beaver Dam.
The freedom of live cover
alluring, he undressed me
in splotchy sunlight, layers
peeling back like damp leaves,
my hands curling to his mouth
like trilliums on a mossy bed,
his heat flush with the sky.

Despite that woodsy sheet of honeysuckle
air, the chorus of chickadees, the earth
warm as stones in an open stream,
I could not remove the strain
of my father's shoulders hugging the cliff,
Lady panting in his arms, my own
small feet worrying their way upward,
new with knowing he had misjudged
the world, or I, his aim.
I look for the beaver now,
their gray wash of work. Interlocking
vines stifle the path, a small voice
squeezed to unending silence, the late
October berries dark with juice,
my father's first failure
smarting in my hand.

***

"Impelled Toward the Light" was previously published in *Earth's Daughters, 33/34*, 94–96, 1989. Republished with permission.

Winning Ways
Carl "Papa" Palmer

I taught him competition,
always be the star,
play to win,

excel in my eyes,
make dad proud,
best in his class,

stay on top,
maintain that edge,
all this well learned

as he slung those damn darts
at the damn rec room wall,
stormed up those damn stairs

slammed that damn door
when I beat him to the bull's eye
the second time in a row.

Night Fears

By Louis Hoffman

You would not go to sleep
those long nights
Unless I lay by your bed
On the cold hard floor
A blanket too small
trying to keep me warm

Sometimes you'd talk
and I'd listen a while
before saying,
"Now go to sleep,"
with late night work
beckoning below

The light moved slowly
on the ceiling as
cars drove by
Some nights, a fox
would call out
like a crying baby
Some nights it was
just the stars and the wind

Then one evening,
after your brother
was born, you went to sleep
without me. I sat
in my computer's soft glow
missing the uncomfortable nights
where my mere presence
allayed your fears.

Climbing the stairs to your room
I saw your face in the soft moonlight
touching your head gently
and watching your chest move

For a moment, all my fears
were gone.

Poetry Activities

Poetry Activity 1: Photographic Inspiration
Find a photo of your child or parent that has meaning for you. Spend 3–5 minutes looking at the photo, noticing what comes to mind. It could be memories, stories, emotions, or sensations. As you reflect on this, find a focus that comes forth that can serve as an inspiration for a poem.

Poetry Activity 2: Earliest Memory
Many poems in *Lullabies and Confessions* focus on early memories of one's parent or early memories after a child was born. Try to recollect one of your earlier memories of one of your parents or children. As you reflect on this memory, notice what is most salient about the memory. Allow this to become a poem.

Poetry Activity 3: A Week of Memories
Identify one of your parents or children that you would like to focus on (you can repeat this several times to include all your parents and/or children if you would like). For a week, immerse yourself in memories of this person. This can include looking through old photographs, reading back through old letters, talking with other friends and family members about stories about the person, and spending time each day reflecting on fond memories. It can also include conversations with the person. As you do this, you can write poems along the way or wait until you have spent a week with memories and then write a poem inspired from this week of immersion. If you write several poems over the course of the week, read back through them at the end and reflect on how they evolved over the week and how they fit together. This may involve holding very different experiences and emotions together.

Poetry Activity 4: Poetic Letter
Poems, at times, can take a narrative form, whether a narrative poem or not. Identify a child or parent with whom you have something important to share that you have kept to yourself. Write a poem to them. This poetic letter can be in any style that you would like. Often, it can help to find music that is connected thematically to what you

want to share or to the emotions related to what you want to share. You can listen to this song or a collection of songs to try to intensify the emotions before you sit down to write the poem. It is not necessary to share this poem with the other person and, generally, it is best to not consider sharing during the writing process to allow yourself greater freedom of expression.

Poetry Activity 5: As a Child, As a Parent
This activity intends to explore the connection of your experience of your parents with your experience as a parent. There are two parts to this exercise that parallel each other. Use the line prompts below to begin a line or several lines:

> As a child, I....
> I experienced...
> I learned...
> I now am...
>
> As a parent, I...
> I experienced...
> I learned...
> I now am...

You may begin your first version of the poem with the words from the prompts included. However, you can use the theme of these lines while altering the words. Or, after writing your first draft, return and alter the words to allow greater freedom of expression. After you have finished this exercise, spend some time reflecting or journaling on how your experience as a child and as a parent connect.

Poetry Activity 6: Exploring Conflict
Relationships of depth inevitably will encounter conflict. Identify a conflict that you have had with your parent or with one of your children. Spend time reflecting on this, trying to get in touch with the emotions you experienced at the time of the conflict. Begin the poem trying to vividly describe the conflict or an aspect of the conflict, such as your emotional or visceral experience. After finishing this, set the poem aside for a while. This may be 5–10 minutes or later in the day or next day. Return to the poem and read it again. Now, reflect on anything you learned from the conflict. After reflecting on this, write another poem, or a continuation of the poem, that focuses on the

lessons you learned from the conflict.

Poetry Activity 7: Lessons of Time
Identify a parent or one of your children whom you would like to focus on with this activity. Spend some time reflecting or journaling about how the relationship has changed over time, paying particularly attention to milestones or events that brought about change. Next, try to identify a symbol or metaphor that represents the change or changes in the relationship over time. After you have identified these, begin writing a poem that utilizes the symbol or metaphor of change.

Poetry Activity 8: A Poem a Day
Identify a period of time in which you will try to read a poem a day. We recommend this being a minimum of one week. Read at least one poem a day from *Lullabies & Confessions*. If reading through in order and you do not connect with a poem you read on a particular day, then read a couple more poems until you find one that you can connect with. If you have already read *Lullabies & Confessions* and marked your favorites, you may just read back through your favorites. After you have read each poem, journal about it or reflect on what you connect with in that poem. Pay particular attention to any emotions that emerge from reading the poem and what those emotions may be telling you.

About the Editors

Louis Hoffman, PhD, is a licensed psychologist practicing in Colorado Springs and offering TelePsychology (online therapy) in various states. He serves as the Executive Director of the Rocky Mountain Humansitic Counseling and Psychological Association (www.rmhcpa.org) and the Associate Director of the International Institute for Existential–Humanistic Psychology (www.iiehp.org). Dr. Hoffman has been recognized as a Fellow of the American Psychological Association and six of its divisions (1, 10, 32, 36, 48, & 52) for his contributions to professional psychology. An avid writer, Dr. Hoffman has edited/authored 18 books and over 100 journal articles and book chapters. His books include *Our Last Walk: Using Poetry for Grieving and Remembering Our Pets*; *Stay Awhile: Poetic Narratives on Multiculturalism and Diversity*; *Humanistic Approaches to Multiculturalism and Diversity;* and *Existential Psychology East–West* (Volumes 1 & 2). He serves on the editorial boards of the *Journal of Humanistic Psychology* (Senior International Editor), *The Humanistic Psychologist*, the *Journal of Constructivist Psychology,* and *Janus Head*. Although Dr. Hoffman left fulltime academia to pursue private practice and his passion for writing, he continues to teach at the University of Denver, the University of Colorado at Colorado Springs, and Saybrook University. Most important, Dr. Hoffman is a father, a husband, and a son who is blessed with a wonderful, loving family. He enjoys living in the beautiful mountains of Colorado with his family and two dogs. For more information about Dr. Hoffman's writing, visit his website at www.louis-hoffman.com.

Lisa Xochitl Vallejos, PhD, is a licensed professional counselor in Colorado. She is the current Board Chair of the Rocky Mountain Humanistic Counseling and Psychological Association as well as the President and co-founder of The Humanitarian Alliance. She serves on a number of boards and has been involved in many community task forces and initiatives. She currently teaches Anti-Racist, Anti-Oppression, and Social Justice trainings for mental health professionals. Dr. V is the author of *Shattered: How Everything Came Together When it All Fell Apart* and is an author or co-author on a number of articles and book chapters. Dr. V offers transpersonal perspectives on relationships, parenting, and life. She currently lives in Colorado with her two children and puppy, Goliath. For more information, please visit her website at www.lisavallejos.com

For information about the contributors, please visit:
www.universityprofessorspress.com/poetry-healing-and-growth-series-contributors

www.ingramcontent.com/pod-product-compliance
Lightning Source LLC
Chambersburg PA
CBHW050552160426
43199CB00015B/2632